"Guests want to come back [to church] because of what they experience during their first visit. How to make that happen is what Jason and Jonathan share in this book."

From the foreword by **Andy Stanley**

"Jason Young and Jonathan Malm have written an important book for anyone hoping to grow their church, expand their ministry, or strengthen their business. In *The Come Back Effect*, they give the reader practical ways to create a healthy and thriving culture."

Craig Groeschel, pastor, Life.Church; author, *Divine Direction: 7 Decisions That Will Change Your Life*

"Hospitality is, in its simplest form, the loving of strangers. This book dives deep in showing what that looks like. Read and prepare for impact."

Dr. Johnny Hunt, senior pastor, First Baptist Church Woodstock

"I'm not sure most churches—or businesses, for that matter—pay close enough attention to the power of hospitality in ministry and business. Jason and Jonathan provide leaders with a great framework for creating amazing experiences for first-time and returning guests!"

Tyler Reagin, president, Catalyst

"This is one of the best books I've read when it comes to guest experience and hospitality at a church. Reading through this book made me think of different ways to train my volunteers and how they see and engage with our guests."

Rommel ? ┤dleback Church

"To get a guest t┊ ┊siness, providing care and deli┊ ┊ry experience. Jason and Jonat┊ ┊nal stories and practical steps ar┊ ┊ need to read."

Horst Schulze, founder and CEO, Capella Hotels; founder, Ritz-Carlton Hotels

"Service comes from a manual; hospitality comes from the heart. In *The Come Back Effect*, Jason and Jonathan unpack how gracious hospitality and generosity of spirit will lead to a powerful, lasting relationship between people and your church or business."

Kirk Kinsell, former president and CEO, Loews Hotels; former president, Intercontinental Hotels Group (Americas)

"The environment we create for our guests, team members, and regular attendees speaks to the focus and heart of the organization. Jason and Jonathan clearly articulate, in a practical manner, a framework that ensures everything communicates a loving embrace for all who open the doors."

Paul Bowers, president and CEO, Georgia Power

"How do we take the best knowledge from companies like hotels and restaurants and bring that excellence to the church? I'm excited to see this conversation in the church. Jason and Jonathan give us the tools to create loving, welcoming environments that draw people to the love of Christ."

Cheryl Bachelder, former CEO, Popeyes Louisiana Kitchen Inc.; author, *Dare to Serve*

"Every single person in ministry needs to read *The Come Back Effect*. Whether your ministry is already bringing people back in droves or you have a long way to go, this book will help you go farther faster. Read this book—and watch your ministry go to the next level."

Luis Martinez-Soto, volunteer development director, Lakewood Church

"It's easy to be become disconnected from what it's like to be a guest. Jason and Jonathan have written an inspiring and helpful book that puts us back in the shoes of our guests and reminds us what matters most. This book is not just for your greeters; it will empower your entire team to create a dynamic weekend experience at church. I will be referencing and recommending this book often."

Brandon Stewart, director, Team Church Conference

"Truett Cathy taught me, 'Hospitality is cheap, but it pays great dividends.' Creating a culture of hospitality is vital for our restaurants and any team that wants to fulfill its purpose. Jason and Jonathan provide a powerful guide to help you create a culture! My hope is this book impacts you at a heart level, where it affects how you serve not only on Sunday but every day!"

Chris Darley, owner/operator, Chick-fil-A, Atlanta, Georgia

THE COME BACK EFFECT

HOW HOSPITALITY CAN COMPEL
YOUR CHURCH'S GUESTS TO RETURN

JASON YOUNG AND JONATHAN MALM

BakerBooks

a division of Baker Publishing Group
Grand Rapids, Michigan

© 2018 by Jason Young and Jonathan Malm

Published by Baker Books
a division of Baker Publishing Group
PO Box 6287, Grand Rapids, MI 49516-6287
www.bakerbooks.com

Printed in the United States of America

Library of Congress Cataloging-in-Publication Data
Names: Young, Jason, 1978– author. | Malm, Jonathan, author.
Title: The come back effect : how hospitality can compel your church's guests to
    return / Jason Young and Jonathan Malm.
Description: Grand Rapids, MI : Baker Books, a division of Baker Publishing
    Group, [2018] | Includes bibliographical references.
Identifiers: LCCN 2017059999 | ISBN 9780801075780 (pbk.)
Subjects: LCSH: Hospitality—Religious aspects—Christianity. | Church. | Church
    attendance.
Classification: LCC BV4647.H67 Y68 2018 | DDC 253/.7—dc23
LC record available at https://lccn.loc.gov/2017059999

The authors are represented by the literary agency of The Blythe Daniel Agency, Inc.

Some names and details have been changed to protect the privacy of the individuals involved.

18 19 20 21 22 23 24   7 6 5 4 3 2 1

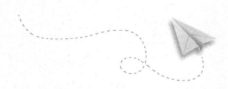

For the guests coming to your church this weekend.
They're about to feel loved like never before.

Contents

Foreword

I recently read a letter from a woman who had been so persistent in inviting her children to attend our church that her husband asked her to stop pressuring them to come. They were adults who had developed a strong distaste for church and for Christians. When she finally leveraged all of her influence to get them to attend with her for Christmas, it was under the stipulation that she would have to sit through lunch afterward and listen to *their* thoughts on faith.

In her letter, she described in great detail their experience at one of our campuses. She remembered names, hand gestures, and even the facial expressions of our guest services volunteers and the people onstage. She noticed all those things because she was extra sensitive to the experience. It wasn't just her perspective that mattered this time; she was seeing the service through the eyes of her family. After the service, the verdict came in. *The experience was excellent.* One of her children even commented that the "customer service" was better than at the Hyatt.

The end result was a completely different conversation at lunch. Instead of a religious debate, they discussed the excellence they had just experienced. They felt like the experience had been tailored to them. One of her children—known to be a cynic, debater, and atheist—described what he experienced at church that day as a "10"!

When I was asked to write the foreword for this book, I thought about that letter. What this woman experienced isn't uncommon for those who attend a North Point Ministries church. Her children had felt pressure from their mom because of their differing views toward church and Christians. But instead of the experience adding to that pressure, it actually alleviated it. It began to change their feelings about church and maybe even God. *That's the "come back effect."* Guests want to come back because of what they experience during their first visit. How to make that happen is what Jason and Jonathan share in this book.

I have the privilege of working personally with Jason as he focuses on instilling the come back effect in our guest services staff and volunteers. He gets it. He feels what our guests feel, and he brings that awareness to our weekend experiences. I've also seen how he invests in our volunteers. How he cares for them affects how they care for our guests.

Jason and Jonathan both see that what can become routine for us is extremely personal to our guests. There's no "typical Sunday," because each Sunday is important to the people who are visiting that week.

We've seen these principles at work throughout North Point Ministries. They don't just impact one team; they impact the entire organization. As Jason has tested these principles and shared his expertise with our other guest services directors, his ideas have become further refined at all our campuses.

I recommend you take this opportunity to get a glimpse into the "why" behind *The Come Back Effect*. This book isn't just a series of nice ideas. We've seen firsthand how the principles within open the hearts of our guests to Jesus and transform their lives. And that's why we do this, right?

Andy Stanley
Author, communicator, and founder
of North Point Ministries

Acknowledgments

Jason would like to thank:

Andy Stanley, for being a leader worth following.

North Point Ministries, for being a place that cares for guests and volunteers and yet still tries to learn new ways to become remarkable.

Buckhead Church Guest Services volunteers, for being a team who prioritizes elevating the dignity of the guest.

Lance Martin, for being a close friend and someone who tells me like it is. You are in my corner and there have been many days I've needed it.

Jeff Jackson, Brooklynn Warren, Rhonda Hinrichs, Rebecca Parrish, and Patrick Riesenberg, for being a team that believes in what we do seven days a week. I'm proud of you.

Chris Green, for being a leader who believed in me and trusted me from the beginning.

My wife, Stacy, for giving me the space to dream and write. If people only knew how much you support me.

My parents, for being voices who cheer me on.

Debbie Miller, for being a prayer warrior more days than I can even count.

Pastor Johnny Hunt, for being the first person to invite me in and trust me at FBC Woodstock to create remarkable environments for volunteers and guests.

Jonathan would like to thank:

Grace Avenue Church, for being our guinea pig and letting us test the material on your leadership team.

Blythe Daniel, for "getting" this project when others in the industry didn't. You approached the product with creativity and optimism.

Authors' Note

We come from pretty different organizational backgrounds but share a similar passion. Jason works at North Point Ministries as well as with some of the largest churches and businesses helping them achieve this thing called "the come back effect." Meanwhile, Jonathan works with smaller to medium-sized ministries doing the same.

When we first started brainstorming this project, it was a blast to see how the principles we planned to cover worked in almost any environment—whether small or large, and even ministry or for-profit. We believe the ten big ideas in this book will help you create an environment where guests will feel compelled to come back.

1. Focus on Feeling as Much as Function
2. Create a Culture, Not a Job Title
3. Know the Guest
4. Be Fully Present
5. Think Scene by Scene
6. Recover Quickly

7. Observe Details, Because Everything Communicates

8. Reject "Just Okay"

9. Choose Values over Policies

10. Reach for Significance

When we talk about a "guest," we're primarily referring to a first-time visitor to your church. But the way you treat the "guest" shouldn't be that much different depending on whether it's their first or fiftieth time. These principles can be applied to first-timers, volunteers, or even lifelong members of your organization. Whether they attend your church, shop with your business, or attend your small group, applying these principles to the way you deal with guests can give you the come back effect.

Throughout the book we'll share personal stories to help illustrate the principles. To keep things clear, we'll make sure you know whose story is whose. But regardless of which stories belong to which person, we hope you'll start seeing your own ministry (or even business) environment in the narrative. Your organization can become the type that's magnetic—reaching new guests and creating that sticking point where they ultimately return and find their home.

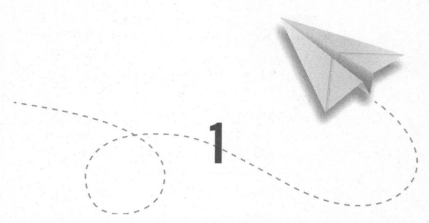

Focus on Feeling as Much as Function

▶ JASON

There's only one thing I regret about my wedding. It was the wedding reception.

I got married in my hometown. My wife, Stacy, is from Oklahoma City. So obviously, we hosted many more of my friends and family at the wedding than hers. And because of that, I was so focused on serving everybody at the reception that I left my wife standing there by herself. I was worried about greeting and hosting everyone, and I neglected to enjoy time with her. I let my service overwhelm what the whole event was all about. To this day, that's the one thing Stacy says she wishes I'd done differently—simply been "with her" at the reception.

I was so focused on the task in front of me that I didn't focus on the person.

■ ■ ■

In many ministries, the guest experiences what Stacy experienced. The service was excellent; not a single task was left incomplete. But the guest feels neglected. They feel *served*, but they don't feel *hospitality*.

Churches love to talk about serving. It's a huge idea that Jesus epitomized. It encapsulates the concepts of humility, compassion, and going the extra mile. Serving is so action oriented. When you hear "serving," it's all about doing something.

Unfortunately, churches have used the term so much that we never really hear about hospitality. We don't ever talk about the feeling. Serving is about doing more and completing tasks. But what happens when serving actually hurts someone's experience?

The quintessential story of Jesus's servant heart was when he washed his disciples' feet. We love to tell that story because that's service at its finest. But we don't really think about the cultural context or what it really meant to the disciples. Foot washing was either something intimate between a husband and wife, or it was something reserved for the lowest servants to do for their masters. It wasn't a normal thing you would see your authority figure doing for you.

Imagine a church that instituted foot washing in their services for first-time guests. The service element would be strong! People would talk about that church! But every single guest who visited the church would feel uncomfortable. How awkward would it be to visit a place for the first time and have a complete stranger wash your feet—bunions, fungus, and all? The church would be serving their guests, but they wouldn't be hospitable about it.

No matter how over-the-top your service, if it doesn't connect with the emotions of the guest, it isn't hospitality. Hospitality is about the feeling.

18

This can be an uncomfortable concept for many modern churches. *Aren't feelings bad? Don't they lie?* Yes, they do lie. That's the point. A business, for instance, wants a product that the customer will love. However, even if the product is perfect, the experience of the store, or the shipping, or the ordering process can all ruin the product—even though they have very little to do with the actual product. Thus, great customer service for a business removes negative emotions from the periphery of their product.

As a church, though, we want to remove the negative emotions that might get in the way of ministry. We aren't trying to manipulate some happy feeling in the hopes someone will come back to our ministry. We're trying to care enough for our guests to replace their negative emotions so real ministry can happen. That's when you start seeing the come back effect—when you care enough about your guests to create an atmosphere where real ministry can take place.

▶ JASON

There's a man who works at the Walmart by my house. He perfectly illustrates this idea of service without hospitality. The first time my wife and I encountered him, I had a simple question about the location of an item in the frozen foods section. He cheerily offered to escort me to the item. But once we found it, he didn't leave. He stood a bit too close to me and started talking to me about completely unrelated topics. His gestures while talking to me felt like an octopus wriggling into my personal space. He didn't simply solve our problem then ask, "Is there anything else?" He overstayed his welcome in an attempt to be over-the-top friendly.

I remember telling my wife as we walked away, "That dude takes his job for real. And I don't mean that in a good way."

Now when we visit that Walmart, we don't ask this guy for help, because he goes so above and beyond that it actually ruins the experience.

■ ■ ■

Hospitality is about caring for the emotions of the guest just as much as it is about serving them, if not even more. That means knowing when it's time to go above and beyond the call of duty or when it's time to walk away. Hospitality is about merging the function—the tasks—and the feeling.

Every time a guest experiences us, we should honor them enough to deliver the same level of hospitality in every experience. But that same level of hospitality might mean responding differently each time, because the experience is about the guest. It's not about making ourselves feel good about the service we provided. It's making the guest feel good about the hospitality we showed.

Many ministries have been "doing" this serving thing for so long that all they worry about is "doing." We need to reimagine what it means to be the guest and what it means to add feeling back into it. This means prioritizing the feelings of the guest over the tasks we perform for them.

There's a story in Luke 10 where Jesus visits the house of a woman named Martha. She invited Jesus into her home and, being the good hostess, was busy preparing a dinner in the kitchen. Meanwhile, her sister, Mary, was simply sitting with Jesus and conversing with him.

Martha complained to Jesus about this. "Can you tell my lazy sister to help me prepare the meal instead of lounging out here with you?"

She expected Jesus to have her back and instruct Mary to help with the tasks. But he reminded Martha of the value of being with someone. Martha was so busy *serving* Jesus that she neglected to *be with* Jesus. How many of our team members are so busy *serving* our guests that they neglect to simply *be with* our guests? Imagine if Martha had spent more time with Jesus. Imagine if she had merged the function and the feeling of what she was doing. She might have brought the bowls and ingredients into the room where Jesus was sitting. She might have even explained what she was doing, bringing the relationship into the function.

How does this play out in our ministries?

Parking attendants can get so busy simply parking cars that they forget there's a real person behind that driver's-side window or a family experiencing their own stresses. When parking cars becomes a service, you might see the attendant talking to a friend while gesturing to the nearest open spot. Or the attendant might look a bit uncomfortable in the heat of the summer day. You can tell it's more about the function than about hospitality for the parking lot attendant.

Hospitality looks different. It acknowledges feelings. As a person looks for a parking spot, they are experiencing feelings. They might be feeling anxious, confused, or overwhelmed in this new place. A parking lot attendant who gets what the guest is feeling will make subtle changes to his approach. He'll still park the cars, but he might make the following changes:

- His gestures will be slower.
- He'll be more patient when people don't quickly make it to the spot he's guiding them to.
- He won't be as sharp.
- He'll make eye contact with the driver.
- He'll notice the children in the back seat and wave at them with a smile.

- His facial expressions will be gentle and warm.
- He'll notice the tire pressure is low and offer to fill the tire or change it for the guest during the service.

He'll realize that the feeling he can give the guest is even more important than the task he's performing. He realizes that people respond to feeling and that feeling is memorable. His job is not to park cars; it's to show hospitality to the guest through the act of parking cars. To be honest, the guest could probably find their own parking spot. But if the parking lot attendant is able to ease the stress the driver is feeling, then he performed a valuable function. He (or she) delivered hospitality.

Think of a time you visited a new church or a business. You probably had an impression of the place, and you formed a decision to stay away from the place or visit again. There are times we can pinpoint why we like a church or a business. But there are other times we aren't sure *why* we liked or disliked a place. It's just something we felt.

There will be people who will return to your church and won't know why. They simply felt good there. And there will be others who won't be coming back. They can't explain to someone who asks why they decided not to return; it was just a feeling.

Feelings are important—often even more important than the function. That's why we must merge the two.

The question to ask when faced with this information is obvious: Do we simply let the tasks go in exchange for the feeling? No. This idea of merging function and feeling is about a perspective shift more than anything. It's not strictly a behavioral change, though this *will* affect your behavior. It's about focusing on the feeling of the task—not simply the task itself.

▶ JONATHAN

There's a coffee shop I visit frequently. I'm a bit of a regular there; they always make my coffee right. I respect that they do their job well. But one of the things that made this particular coffee shop my favorite was one simple thing. At some point, each of the baristas moved beyond merely making my coffee to becoming my friend. They began asking my name and asking about my job. In the moment they ask details about me, it feels like they're stepping outside of their role and making a personal connection with me. It's that feeling they've injected into my visit.

Don't get me wrong; if they continually messed up my drink order, it wouldn't matter how personal our connection. I probably wouldn't keep coming back. The function has to be there. But the merging of the feeling and the function makes the coffee shop excellent.

■ ■ ■

When the emotion is there, it doesn't feel like someone's doing their job. It's like they're your friend. It feels like they're rooting for you and that doing their job is a way to support you—not just a means to perform a task.

Connecting with the Existing Feeling

Empathy is one of the most important elements of hospitality— understanding and acknowledging what the guest is feeling. A typical guest experiences many feelings during a visit to a church or business, and many of them are not good. Understanding those feelings is vital to a successful guest experience. But understanding is not enough. Excellence in hospitality means replacing those existing negative feelings.

A guest who is visiting a church may already be feeling anxious, nervous, confused, agitated . . . Maybe the traffic was bad. Maybe they feel overwhelmed by the large size of the building. Maybe they feel like all eyes are on them because of the small size of the building. Maybe they've had a bad experience in the past with church—so they're already coming out fighting.

If we remember those possibilities, what we deliver has the opportunity to replace that emotion. We could replace a bad emotion with a positive emotion.

Imagine a first-time guest who arrives to the service a little bit late. Now, an usher's default task is to fill the auditorium seats from the front to the back. It looks good on camera and makes the pastor feel good about the room. So the usher spots the first-timer and ushers them all the way to the front row and seats them (because all the regulars sat in the back instead of pushing their way to the front).

How do you think the first-time guest feels? They could probably die of embarrassment! People are staring at them. They feel stupid that they're late. And nobody understands they're late because their young child threw up on them that morning right before getting into the car.

Because the usher didn't connect with the current emotion the guest was experiencing, he further compounded the bad feeling the guest had. He missed out on the opportunity to replace it with a positive emotion.

What if, instead, the usher approached it a different way? He could ask, "Would you like to sit in the front or the back? I have an amazing spot up front if you want, or I could get you a prime seat in the back." Because the usher is on top of his function, he's identified all the empty seats. But because the usher has connected with what the guest might be feeling, he's taken their preference into account. Then, if possible, he gets them to their preferred seat. That acknowledges the emotion of the first-time guest.

Then, if the usher wanted to replace that emotion the guest was experiencing, he would take it a step further. He'd usher them to their seat in a relaxed manner—matching the pace of the guest—and introduce the first-time guest to the individual they'd be sitting by. Even if no names were exchanged, a simple "enjoy the service" to both of them would help break the tension the guest and the person they're sitting by might be feeling. It would be like a seal of approval on this guest that they shouldn't be embarrassed for arriving late—a nonverbal welcome: "We value the fact that you took time out of your day to be with us. We're honored you are here."

The original emotion was embarrassment and urgency. The replacement emotion was dignity and peace. You can bet the guest would remember that feeling when they thought back on whether they wanted to visit the church for a second time.

The role of hospitality is to protect how the guest feels and to give them the best possible experience.

Becoming a Broker

We're all familiar with the idea of a bodyguard. In fact, you've probably seen a dramatic scene in a movie where a gunshot rings out. The film speed slows down as the brave bodyguard hurls himself in front of the person he's protecting. His body inches in front of the bullet, which then makes its impact. The film speeds up, chaos ensues, and you see the relief on the protected person's face. The bodyguard saved their life by taking the bullet. The brave protector considered the life of their client more important than their own.

While it's not going to be quite so dramatic, that's essentially the role our teams should take for their guest. They are a shield—a bodyguard for the guest. They broker bad experiences so the guest doesn't have to experience them. For example, when a team member sees themselves as a broker:

- The guest doesn't have to feel lost when they can't find their car. The parking lot attendant takes that emotion on themselves and finds it for them.
- The guest doesn't have to feel embarrassed when their child throws up in the children's room. The childcare worker takes that emotion on themselves and cleans it up.
- The guest doesn't have to feel confused when they're trying to find out the time of a support group that meets at the church. The greeter takes that feeling, absorbs it, and does the legwork to find out for the guest.

Brokering the experience for the guest is about sheltering them from the emotion. It's jumping in front of the uncomfortable bullet and absorbing that so the guest doesn't have to experience it.

▶ JASON

A single mother came into our services looking for a seat. She requested a seat at the end of a row so she could quickly slip out in the event that her child needed attention during the service. An usher found a row where this might be possible and asked a woman who was already seated, "Ma'am, would it be possible for you to scoot down? This lady needs an aisle seat this morning."

The woman in the seat looked down, then back up and said, "She can walk around me."

The usher apologetically looked at the guest, walked her away from the seat, and said, "I'm sorry, ma'am. If you would like to sit in an aisle seat, you don't have to sit there because that doesn't feel like the most enjoyable place to sit." Then he escorted her to another seating area.

If the usher had said nothing or seated her next to the inconsiderate lady, the guest would have been left feeling the embarrassment and shame of the situation. But because he acknowledged the situation and protected the guest, she felt empowered again. She felt comfortable and respected.

■ ■ ■

What a powerful thing when we can broker the experience for our guests! When we acknowledge what they're feeling and work to protect them from that, we make a guest feel truly honored.

In fact, you can even use language like that. It disarms a guest when you say something like:

- "I'll keep you from feeling embarrassed."
- "I don't want you to feel lost."
- "You got here at the perfect time!"

We never want to reinforce a guest's insecurities. Instead, we want to reinforce their security. Their comfort. Their confidence. Those emotions are memorable and will stick with the guest long after their visit is over.

Brokering the guest's feelings is our way in the small scale to reflect what Christ did for us on the large scale. In Isaiah 53:4, the Bible describes Jesus as having borne our sorrows and anxieties. He took them on himself so we no longer had to. While we could never match the sacrifice Jesus made for us, the come back effect is one small way we can follow Jesus's example—to shoulder our guests' burdens for them.

What a Guest Should Feel

Each day, ask yourself two questions to get this idea of hospitality stirring around in your head.

1. **Today, how do you want your guests to feel?** Then ask, in the moment, how you can encourage a guest to feel the way you've decided you want them to feel.

2. **How do you want your team members to feel today?** Understand that the way a team member feels directly affects how they will make the guest feel. You shouldn't expect your team to take care of a guest if they don't feel cared for by the church or the team. Put wind in the sails of your teammates—because that's what they're going to do for the guest.

What do you want your guests to feel? What do you want them to *not* feel? Determine in your heart and with your team how you will get the guest to feel the good feelings and stay away from the bad feelings. For instance, if you're a small group leader, figure out what you want your guests to feel as they enter the classroom or your home. Do you have enough seats; will it be obvious to the guest you were expecting them and prepared? Is it clear where your guest needs to go—easy to identify the classroom or house?

If you're a team leader, expose your team both to the good and to the negative feelings so they can know what good feelings to deliver in order to replace the negative emotion. Train your team to become experts on intentionally delivering positive feelings in a manner similar to how bankers are trained to deal with counterfeit money: know the fake exists, but only deal with the real so you know when you see and feel the fake. In other words, know that negative feelings happen, but show the team what's possible.

Check out this list below and highlight the positive feelings that stick out to you. Then underline the negative feelings you've experienced in guest services environments.

You want your guests to feel

- confident
- safe
- satisfied
- accepted
- hopeful
- acknowledged
- empowered
- educated

- pleased
- comfortable
- excited
- interested
- valued
- relaxed
- welcomed
- familiar

- included
- refreshed
- challenged
- secure
- in control
- delighted

You don't want your guests to feel

- confused
- unsafe
- skeptical
- cynical
- suspicious
- ignored
- annoyed

- doubtful
- angry
- hurt
- distrustful
- processed
- rushed
- uneasy

- frustrated
- uninitiated
- overwhelmed
- uncomfortable
- out of control
- helpless

► JASON

One Sunday, there was a woman standing by guest services. A volunteer, Tracy, took the opportunity to engage her in a conversation. "Are you waiting for family members? Friends?"

The woman replied, "No, I just lost my three-month-old baby. I had no other place to go, so I came to church. But my husband wouldn't come with me."

Tracy knew another guest services volunteer named Carter who had also lost his son. She took the woman over to the man and introduced her. She didn't tell her that Carter had also experienced a similar loss, but she knew that he would have empathy that was needed for the situation.

Carter then invited the lady to sit with him in the service. "I'm not sure I'll be able to make it through the service," she said.

Carter replied, "That's okay. I'll be here as long as you want to stay."

She stayed the entire time. Afterward, she talked to one of our team members and joined a women's group.

■ ■ ■

The function of these volunteers wasn't any extra than normal. But because they focused on the feeling as much as the function, it made all the difference in this lady's life. She could feel the empathy through their interactions.

Life is so hurried. It's so hectic. What if church could be the place where a guest feels the least hurried? Where the relational moments could provide a safe environment—safe to process through the most difficult moments in our life? Hospitality—connecting feeling and function—is the first step in creating the come back effect.

KEY POINTS and TAKEAWAYS

1. Serving is task oriented; hospitality is feeling oriented. Simply performing tasks is not enough to compel a guest to come back.

2. Hospitality should change the way we perform our tasks. Tasks are important, but it's the intangible feelings we transmit that turn them into moments of hospitality.

3. People *will* be feeling something when they arrive to your ministry (stress, nervousness, or confusion). Our job in the come back effect is to replace those negative emotions with positive ones.

4. Great hospitality is shielding the guest from negative experiences by throwing ourselves in front of the situation—like a bodyguard takes a bullet for the one they're protecting.

5. Decide proactively what you want your guests to feel, then look for ways to create environments that will help them experience that.

6. Imagine if your ministry was the least-hurried moment of your guest's week. That could be the ultimate thing to compel them to return.

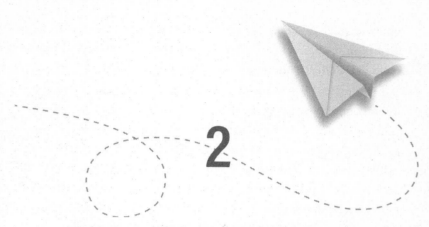

Create a Culture, Not a Job Title

Culture. What a buzzword! You hear it everywhere in both the business world and the church world. But what does it even mean? What is a culture, and what does it mean when you apply it to guest services?

Simply put, *culture* is the identity of a people group. It's who they are. This encompasses their art, food, entertainment, traditions, and so on. When you add all those things together, you get a group's culture.

► JONATHAN

As a kid, I grew up in the mountains of Central America. My parents were missionaries in the small country of Guatemala. We lived near the city, but most of our ministry happened in tiny villages that you traversed dirt roads to reach. The Malm family, including their three kids, would drive their blue-and-silver Suburban over bumpy roads to work in orphanages and feeding centers in these

33

impoverished villages. Part of this ministry also involved going into families' homes and visiting with them—getting to know them and understanding their culture.

On our first visit to one of these homes, we noticed something interesting. We entered the small cinder-block home with poor ventilation and dirt for flooring. We saw the man of the house fish in his pocket for a few *quetzales* (Guatemalan currency) and call his son over. The young child took the money from his dad and then ran outside barefoot across the village to a local *tienda* (a small refreshment kiosk). A few minutes into our conversation, the boy returned with some ice-cold bottles of Coca-Cola—one for each of us. We tried to insist that we weren't thirsty and that they didn't need to do this for us. We knew it was probably a financial stretch to provide five bottles of Coke for our family. But they insisted, and we eventually gave in.

We noticed this at each subsequent house we visited. Each time the parents sent one of their children to buy their honored guests a Coke. We found out through our years of ministry that this is what they do in these Guatemalan villages. It was their way of welcoming guests into their home. It had become part of their identity. It was their culture.

■ ■ ■

Hospitality can't just be a job title at your church. It's not just the team's job to provide hospitality to new guests. Instead, it needs to be a cultural element of your church. A shared value. These Guatemalan families didn't have to think about what they would do when a guest visited them. It was already ingrained in the family that you send your kid running to the nearest *tienda* to buy a Coca-Cola for your guest.

When something becomes part of the culture in your organization, there is a clarity of understanding. It's seen in everything and everyone. There's no discussion or debate. There's no negotiation. Everyone knows what to do, and they do it consistently.

Also, when something becomes part of the culture, it's portable and memorable. That "Coca-Cola for a guest" tradition in Guatemala was the same in each house. Whether the family lived in a small house or in a large house, they still did it. Whether the guest was Guatemalan or glow-in-the-dark white like the Malm family . . . Something that's cultural is easy to pass along and easy to act on. It was valued from generation to generation—old to young.

You can say something is cultural in your ministry, but if it isn't a shared value that's clear, portable, and memorable, it's not really the culture.

▶ JASON

My friend Thomas recently visited a church in a thriving area. This area was filled with growing churches that could barely control the influx of new guests. But my friend noticed the church he visited was dying, while the churches around it were bursting at the seams.

He observed the flow of the service and the people who attended to see if he could identify the issue. The Sunday morning ministry was excellent. That wasn't the problem. But he noticed as soon as the service was over, nearly everyone bolted for the doors and went to their favorite restaurants to eat with their friends. There were only a few volunteers from the guest services team at the doors to talk with the new visitors. None of the volunteers or church regulars wanted to hang around and meet new people.

The church thought they were welcoming. They offered a welcome from the stage. They had a team that held doors for guests.

And they offered a meet-and-greet with the pastor after the service. But that wasn't enough to provide a welcoming atmosphere for new guests. For this church, hospitality was merely a department. It hadn't infiltrated their culture as a church. And it was obvious to my friend Thomas.

■ ■ ■

You see, your ministry or business has a culture, whether you know it or not. And that culture might not be what you hope it is. Your culture is how your people—employees, congregation members, volunteers—*actually* behave.

For instance, the above church wanted to be a welcoming church. They programmed it into their services. They even had a "welcome team" who was responsible for welcoming guests. But it hadn't become part of the DNA of the church. It didn't make its way into the volunteers' and attendees' hearts. It hadn't become part of the culture of that church. Their culture was to swiftly leave and visit with their friends each Sunday at their restaurant of choice.

When guest services becomes part of the culture at your organization, you'll notice it has these four elements:

1. It's pervasive.
2. It's an identity.
3. It's valued from the top down.
4. It's valued with resources.

Let's take the rest of the chapter to look at these four things in more depth. Examine your own church and see if hospitality is merely a department of your church or a culture.

Culture Is Pervasive

We see news stories each year of storms ravaging different areas of the world. Whether a tiny island in the Pacific gets hit by a tsunami or a South American city gets obliterated by an earthquake, these stories tug at our hearts. But what's most profound about these stories is the way the local area responds to these tragedies. You see neighboring cities and countries lending aid. They send envoys with food, water, and relief supplies. They all chip in to help the victims recover from the event.

That's the thing about storms. No matter how isolated they are, they affect nearly everyone. Whether your house stood or fell during the cataclysm, you felt the effects of its power. It reaches you, and you can't help but respond to the event.

That's the sort of thing we're talking about when we say a culture of hospitality is pervasive. There aren't just a couple of people in the ministry who feel the burden to provide hospitality; it impacts the whole team. Everyone sees their personal responsibility to take part and to chip in.

How do you know when a culture of hospitality has pervaded your organization? You'll see it go beyond the confines of your building or events and get into people's everyday lives. Some of the best service organizations witness this phenomenon.

For instance, it's well-known that Chick-fil-A trains their employees to respond with "my pleasure" when somebody thanks them. If you haven't noticed this, visit a Chick-fil-A and thank them when you receive your order. Inevitably they'll respond with "my pleasure." This response has become part of the culture of Chick-fil-A—so much so, in fact, that you'll hear employees say it when they aren't even working. You can actually spot someone who has worked at Chick-fil-A when you hear that response. It's a telltale sign.

That's an indication that hospitality has become part of the culture for an organization—when the behaviors and values transcend the confines of the job. It's not just a program or a department. It's an attitude that works its way into people's everyday lives. It begins to influence how they respond to people—at church, at work, and at home.

A culture that strongly values hospitality begins when people in your ministry react consistently to your guests. Then they start responding to their colleagues the same way. Then to salespeople or restaurant employees. Ultimately it works its way into every circle of their everyday lives. It's no longer something they do. It's who they are.

Culture Reflects an Identity

▶ JASON

Anthony attends one of our North Point Ministries campuses. He's been involved in our guest services team for a number of years in different leadership positions.

One day there was a lady who couldn't find her car. She kept walking in one door and out the other. She was becoming visibly frustrated looking for her vehicle—and dealing with our multiple levels of parking. She was frustrated with herself for not remembering where she parked. Anthony noticed her.

This Sunday, Anthony was done with his responsibilities. He was just about to leave to go home and be with his family. But instead of handing off the responsibility to another guest services volunteer, he spent the next half hour asking some key questions to help her find her vehicle. He was off duty. He had other places to be, but he chose to stay and take care of her. He eventually helped her find her car, and she was so grateful.

I met with Anthony in the middle of the week to talk about how the previous Sunday went, and he relayed this story to me. I praised him and asked him why he would do something like that. His response demonstrated that hospitality was cultural for him—that he gets it.

Anthony responded, "Because that's what we do for people." He explained that this is what he's seen modeled from us. He listens when Pastor Andy Stanley talks. "Do for one what you wish you could do for everyone" comes from every conversation from the team, Andy, and me. It's who we are as a church.

Anthony identified with our cultural value of how we treat people. Then he owned that identity. He saw something that was wrong and he corrected it. Even though it was no longer his responsibility. Even though he was a volunteer. He understood that even though you aren't "on the clock," time doesn't limit when you serve.

■ ■ ■

When hospitality becomes a cultural value instead of just a department, it becomes part of people's identity. It becomes so ingrained in each member of the organization that they're even willing to call it out when others don't model the correct behavior.

▶ JASON

One young couple was visiting, and they asked for directions to the children's environment. The hospitable thing—and what we've taught as part of our culture—is to walk them there. We teach "walk away, walk with." But one of our team members was having an off day and didn't model this behavior. Instead, he said, "Go down the escalators. Take a right. Then go straight, and it's on the right." You can imagine how confusing that might be for a first-time guest.

Fortunately, another team member overheard and decided to take them where they needed to go. He guided them there, conversing with them as they went. It was a small difference, but it had a profound impact on those guests' experience.

The team member who handled the situation approached me after service. "Jason, I need to tell you what happened today."

He explained the situation. It wasn't that the man was being rude or mean. But he realized that's not how our culture operates. It's inconsistent with our identity as an organization.

I immediately talked to the team leader who dropped the ball. He realized he wasn't acting within the culture of our organization. "I know why it happened, but that's not good enough because that's not us."

■ ■ ■

You'll notice that neither man in this story talked in terms of "what they do." They always took it a level deeper to "this is who we are." When a value is strong within your organizational culture, it's no longer about a function, it's about an identity. It's about an identity of empathy.

You'll also notice the immediacy of the correction. If you want something to be part of the culture, it's important to make corrections while the error is still fresh. Don't wait until midweek or the following week when the team member might not remember the situation. If a team member has done this once, maybe that's a reflection of what they believe is acceptable. You don't want that repeated among tens, hundreds, or thousands of guests who visit your ministry. If volunteers are responding incorrectly, either your cultural values haven't infiltrated their identity, or you haven't selected the right people to be part of your team.

A strong culture of hospitality translates to an identity of empathy for your team members. It ceases to be something you do. Instead it becomes something you feel—empathy bleeds into every interaction you have with someone.

Culture Is Valued from the Top Down

▶ JONATHAN

I constantly meet with church workers over coffee. As we dive into the conversation, I frequently hear familiar stories. They feel like cogs in the machine of their church. They feel like they only have value based on their last fifty-hour work week, causing them to feel more like a transaction than a valued individual.

This manifests itself in discouragement and burnout. Their leadership asks for long hours and under-resources the team.

Consequently, that's how they begin treating their volunteers. They snub team members who have to take a few weeks off for a family vacation. Or they serve the guest the best, but leave the volunteers feeling ragged and underappreciated. Thus, that's how their volunteers begin treating the guest. It was all under the guise of "serving," but it was really impersonal and transactional. It started from the top.

On the other hand, though, I occasionally meet with church workers who are in healthy environments. Of course the culture isn't perfect—no team is—but there's a sense that leadership wants to empower the team. They support their team with resources. They're kind and caring. And they recognize the team's contributions and look for ways to give back to the team. That bleeds down into the volunteers and then into how the volunteers treat guests.

■ ■ ■

A strong hospitality culture comes from the top down. It isn't enough to tell your team to treat guests with empathy. You must model it for them. St. Anthony of Padua said, "Actions speak louder than words; let your words teach and your actions speak."[1] It's important that you use words to cast vision for your organization's culture. But your actions will give power to those words. Actions transform functions into culture.

When hospitality is valued from the top down, there are other benefits to the ministry or business. A healthy culture can have the power to

- attract more talent to your organization
- deepen engagement and motivation by your team
- increase retention of volunteers and team members
- raise worker satisfaction and performance levels[2]

This doesn't just affect the guest services team. This sort of hospitality culture permeates the whole organization in positive ways. It becomes the culture.

If you're a leader in your organization, you can influence culture through many things. You can make policies, bring in new employees who model proper behavior, set vision or mission statements, and improve the physical environment of the organization. Those are all good, and they should be part of your leadership. But ultimately, the strongest way to influence culture is through leadership, trust, and treating team members with empathy.

Pouring a bit of water over a pyramid might get a little bit of the lower portions wet. But if you want to saturate every level of the pyramid, you have to completely drench the top—so the trickle can reach every area beneath. As a leader, you're the apex of the pyramid. You have to make sure you model your organization's culture enough that there's plenty to reach those below you.

Culture Is Valued with Resources

▶ JONATHAN

My wife loves fitness. She's one of those CrossFit fanatics. Her idea of a good workout is bloody blisters on her hands and a dull ache in her lower back.

I value working out, but I value it in the sense that I think it's a cool thing to do. My idea of working out is going for a light jog when the weather is nice.

I used to tell my wife how much I appreciated and valued her interests. But I refused to pay the $160/month that CrossFit demanded in order for people to join their cult. Yet I was perfectly fine with paying monthly fees for cable, audiobooks, new gadgets, and other toys that were "necessary for my business."

Would you believe my wife wasn't buying it that I valued her interests? She didn't believe I valued her love of CrossFit until I was willing to put my money where my mouth was. Until I put cash on the table, my words were empty.

■ ■ ■

Some say to "put your money where your mouth is," but Matthew 6:21 expresses it like this: "Wherever your treasure is, there the desires of your heart will also be." The point is, you don't really value something until you're willing to put your money behind it.

For many ministries, the come back effect is more of an aspirational value than a present value. They would like to create a compelling environment that makes second- and third-time visits the norm, but they aren't willing to devote the resources necessary to make it happen. The only way an aspirational value becomes a present value is when money backs it up.

Most churches would say they value these three things equally: service production, family ministry / small groups, and making guests feel welcomed. Yet if you looked at their expenditures over the year, percentages might look something more like this:

Service Production: 60%

Family Ministry / Small Groups: 35%

Guest Services: 5%

And you can bet that the staffing ratios would look similar. Yet it takes just as many volunteers—if not more—to make guest services work well at a church.

You see, if your ministry values the come back effect, it will leak over into everything. Your money will go there. You'll staff it. You'll give them priority.

Businesses have long known this principle of putting money where you want the growth. A business doesn't just start spending money on advertising once they have a bit of excess cash. No, they put money into advertising *in order to* get the extra cash. You have to put money into the areas where you want growth.

The crazy thing is that in a church, nobody really cares about the music or the family groups if they had a bad experience walking in or walking out. They probably won't be back if they didn't feel cared for by the people—if hospitality wasn't part of the church culture. And people will see if hospitality isn't in the culture of a church, even in the little things.

Those little things start with how the ministry organizes its priorities.

In a typical church, you might see a staff meeting that looks like this:

Service Director: We need a new display for the back wall so our singers don't have to worry about forgetting the lyrics to the songs on Sunday. It'll cost around $5,000.

Decision Maker: Let's buy it.

Family Ministries Director: We need to buy new curriculum for our kids' ministry and small groups. Our current curriculum is boring and outdated. It will cost $10,000.

Decision Maker: Make it happen!

Guest Services Director: I want to feed all our volunteers on Sunday mornings. I was thinking about catering some sandwiches from a local deli. It should cost $100 each week.

Decision Maker: That sounds like a lot of money. Can we just buy them canned sausages instead?

Okay, perhaps it isn't quite that drastic. But the same sort of attitude happens in churches all around the country.

Show me your budget items, and I'll show you what your organization truly values. If you want hospitality to stop being just a department in your ministry—and if you want it to become a strong cultural value—you need to put your resources there. You need to value it with more than just words.

How a Culture of Hospitality Looks in Different Ministries

A culture of hospitality isn't just something you should see in a church service setting. It should be part of every ministry within

THE COME BACK EFFECT

a church. Here are some "proofs" that the come back effect is active and that hospitality has become part of the culture within different ministries at an organization.

Small Groups

- The leader spends time recapping elements from previous meetings and even inside jokes, so first-timers can feel included in the group dynamic.
- When the seating is nearly full, regulars will gladly offer their seats to newcomers and find their own—rather than leaving it up to the leader or the visitor to figure out.
- When a newcomer comes through the door, people cheerfully greet them and invite them in instead of stopping their conversation and gawking at them.

Youth Groups / Singles Groups

- Regulars seek people who are attending alone and invite them to sit with them.
- Regular attenders see their job as "host" to newcomers—explaining what happens during the service and inviting them to follow them around.

"Meet the Pastor" Classes

- There will be great signage and even people along the way to direct people to a "Fellowship Hall" or other secondary room—showing awareness that it can be scary to navigate to a new room in a new building.
- The class will be more about getting to know the newcomers—empathizing with them—than sharing all about what the church can offer.

Examine your church. Do you see proof of the come back effect in your culture? What about in specific ministries within the church? What can you do to create a culture of hospitality that compels guests to come back and experience more?

KEY POINTS and TAKEAWAYS

1. Hospitality can't be a job title. It should be a ministry-wide reflexive response.

2. Your ministry has a culture, but it's not necessarily going to be what you hope. You have to be intentional about creating a culture of hospitality.

3. A culture of hospitality bleeds into your team members' everyday lives. Hospitality can't just be something that happens one or two hours each week.

4. When something is part of the culture, it is phrased in terms of "who we are" not "what we do."

5. Hospitality is not just how the volunteer treats the guest; it starts with leadership. Hospitality is how leadership treats the staff and how the staff treats the volunteers.

6. Hospitality isn't a part of the culture until money and resources are devoted to it.

3

Know the Guest

In 1 Corinthians, the apostle Paul talked about becoming like those to whom he ministered. When he was with Jews, he behaved like a Jew and followed their practices. When he was with Gentiles, he ignored Jewish law. No matter where he ministered, Paul found common ground with everyone so that he could bring them to Christ (1 Cor. 9:19–23).

How could Paul have done this successfully if he was unaware of who these people were? To find common ground, he had to know them. That went beyond simply knowing their age group, gender, and how they heard about the church. Paul had to understand their customs. He understood their weaknesses. Their worries. Their values. It required real empathy on Paul's part to become like those he wanted to reach.

Paul needed to know more than demographics (age, gender, marital status, stage of life, area of residence, ethnicity)—the types of questions churches like to ask on their guest cards. He needed real, personal information.

Note that there's nothing wrong with knowing demographics. You can get some valuable insights from this type of information. Different ages and different genders tend to behave certain ways. The same is true for those who are affluent or those who are impoverished. But if we want to take our hospitality to the next level, we need to know more. We need to know what the service industry has labeled *psychographic information*.

The term *psychographics* can seem daunting. But quite simply, psychographics are measurements dealing with someone's psychological state.[1] These are things like personality, values, attitudes, interests, and lifestyles.[2]

While demographics might be able to tell you that your congregation is filled with affluent white couples in their forties, you can't rely on believing all wealthy white couples in their forties think and act the same way. For instance, wealthy oil tycoons in Texas think and behave quite differently from wealthy actors in Hollywood. Or wealthy playboys in Miami. Or wealthy estate owners in Maine. While money might be a unifying factor for these four groups, lumping them all in the same category would yield some interesting results.

When you don't know your guest inside and out, you risk faux pas when dealing with them. In 2014, Apple committed this type of psychographic faux pas when they announced their newest iPhone release. In an attempt to create buzz and show appreciation to their iTunes users, they automatically gave every user U2's newest album release. For some users, that meant it automatically downloaded to their phone or their computer. It seemed like a good idea. U2 is about as big as a band can get—they're internationally famous and even revered. But some users responded to the event with outrage. A social media storm ensued, with people complaining that their devices were running out of space or that their security had been violated.

Apple failed to consider the values, attitudes, and interests of their iTunes users. They assumed they knew the user, but they didn't take the time to truly understand them. Apple and U2's generous gesture was taken as a curse.

This is the risk we run when we don't know the guests who grace the parking lots and lobbies, seats and pews of our ministry. What's intended as a gesture of kindness and welcome can be an affront to the guest.

That's why churches that get this "know the guest" practice right learn as much as possible about their guest. They'll know details like what magazines they read, what television shows they watch, and even where they get their news. It's a deeper level of understanding, but it translates to the come back effect.

When you intentionally understand the who and let that inform your why, you inevitably create a more remarkable and targeted experience of hospitality.

How Do You Get This Information?

Companies like Zappos and Amazon rely on psychographic data as if it were a life preserver in a stormy ocean. They rely on consultants and intense market research to get this information, because these companies are highly competitive. One experience that doesn't match a user's values and attitudes can send them running to the competitor.

Fortunately for us, the church world is a bit more forgiving. We don't need to rely on market research and consultants to get the information we need (though it certainly wouldn't hurt).

► JASON

At North Point Ministries, we survey regular attendees and guests once or twice each year. We ask questions like:

"Based on your overall experience, how was it?"

"Would you come back?"

"Would you bring someone with you?"[3]

But more simply than that, we've taken a page out of the Disney playbook when it comes to obtaining psychographic data. We create multiple listening posts—designated eavesdroppers, if you will—throughout the church, and at the end of the weekend experience, I ask my volunteers, "What did you hear today?"

I frequently ask, so my volunteers have begun listening for things like this. I hear, "We kept hearing about the coffee," or "People were frustrated with the temperature in the building," or "Guests inquired about how we choose the pre-service music playlist." This type of information is invaluable in the way that it informs specific psychographic variables. You discover people's values very quickly when you see what areas of frustration arise in your guest services protocols.

■ ■ ■

It's easy to forget that you have your own market analysts in the form of your team members. Don't overlook this fact. Ask people who are interacting with the people you're trying to reach. Your fellow team members will give you the insights and information you need in order to know your guest.

Businesses can get in on this too. It's as simple as priming employees to listen for specific feedback or even ask specific questions of customers.

Some of the questions you can ask your team members and guests are these:

- **What's right?** What functioned properly and made sense for the guest?
- **What's wrong?** Where did we miss the mark?
- **What's missing?** Was the guest expecting something that we didn't anticipate? Coffee? Signage?
- **What's confusing?** What questions do we consistently answer? And what questions take the longest to answer?[4]

Find ways to ask these questions each weekend or after each event.

Begin to collect all this data. As a team, create a profile of your guest so you can begin crafting your hospitality experience to accommodate their psychographic variables.

What Do You Do with Conflicting Data?

▶ JONATHAN

At the growing church where I worked, we had a greeter who caused some concern. She was an older, sweet-grandmother type. She loved greeting guests. But she did it in an unhealthy way. She frequently hugged first-time guests, and even kissed some of our regulars on the cheek.

A few apprehensive staff members brought up the issue in a meeting where we were talking about our hospitality experience. To most of the team, it seemed obvious that this was too much. We would need to ask her to stop. But not all of our team was on board. "I actually really enjoy when I'm greeted by that lady," said one of the staff members. "In fact, I've talked about it with a few of my friends."

I was surprised, because this team member was a young, twenty-something girl. Because of this, we actually came to an impasse on what we should do. We eventually made the decision to tell her she had to stop hugging and kissing, much to my relief. But I imagine if the weather might have been a bit different that day, the decision would have gone the other way. The scales barely tipped in my favor.

■ ■ ■

This story is an example of conflicting data. The truth is, there will always be some people who prefer X while others prefer Y. If you put too much stock in either opinion, it's easy to become reactionary. It's easy to flip-flop on a whim based on anecdotal evidence.

When you get the data from your frontline team members, it's important to submit those stories to an overarching understanding of what you know about people.

Look for volume, patterns, and impact. If 90 percent of people say the same thing consistently, there's a good chance you need to do something about it. Never react to one story from one guest.

Also look for the why or the motive behind the feedback: "Why do you like this?" or "Why don't you like this?" Often these individual stories will relate to a single personal experience. It might remind them of a good experience they had growing up in another church. Or they might have a different family background that made certain social taboos acceptable to them.

Never make knee-jerk reactions to stories or single opinions. Always keep the big picture in mind.

What Do You Do with This Information?

▶ **JASON**

At many of our campuses, we make breath mints available in the lobby and the restrooms. This is yet another way we can make a guest feel comfortable in our building—fresh breath provides a definite confidence boost. For a long time at one of our campuses, we provided those white-and-red peppermints that your grandmother used to carry in her purse.

But based on some psychographic data and a nudge from my boss, we learned those don't really reflect the preferences of our guests, although they didn't verbally say it. Using the data we'd gathered, I changed the type of breath mints we served to a brand-name wintergreen mint.

It was a subtle change, but it reflected a huge difference in the way we welcomed the guest. Previously, we went through about five large bags of the red-and-white mints each month. But after making this change, we started going through about sixty bags each month. Obviously, wintergreen mints reflected our guests' preferences better.

Now, that's a silly example. But that one small detail tells the guest that we see them and we value them.

■ ■ ■

Mints might seem like a nitpicky change to make. But there are larger changes to make using this psychographic data. Some possibilities might include these:

- You provide large windows looking into the children's rooms so parents can feel like there's more security and accountability.

- Your small group is filled with health nuts, so serving pizza is a bad idea.

- Membership classes are filled with people ready to sign on the dotted line from the get-go, so only one class is necessary. Or maybe your people are more apprehensive, so you ease them into it more slowly.

- Youth aren't getting connected to the youth group after attending the service. You start integrating more young people into the greeting team so the invitation becomes more organic.

- You realize parents of infants are nervous about leaving their kids in the nursery, so you get their cell phone number and text them a picture of their smiling little one during the middle of the service. (Distracting them with a reassuring picture might actually be less disruptive than the tears they're imagining.)

Once you know your guest, make changes that reflect them. One of the main determining factors when someone is deciding to come back to a ministry is knowing whether there are people like themselves who attend. Diversity is important—age, race, gender, and socioeconomic status (what we call *demographics*). But first, people want to know they are surrounded by others who think like they do and have similar values (*psychographics*). The cool thing about that is you can have diversity *with* similarities.

When you pick a greeting team or a team of folks to be the front lines of guest interaction, choose people who will empathize and relate to your guests. Give your guests a chance to say, "They're like me."

At one of our campuses, our average attendee is thirty-three years old. And there's one particular door where most of our families with elementary- or middle-school-aged children enter. Knowing that, I've taken demographic and psychographic data and staffed those areas based on what I know to be true of those people. I often staff other fathers or mothers who have elementary- or middle-school-aged children. Or I'll choose warm, grandfather-type people there. It immediately turns an unfamiliar place into a comfortable place, because they know there are people there who can relate with them.

■ ■ ■

The guest wants to see

- someone like them when they enter the door
- someone with an empathetic response because they connect with a particular life cycle (parent, student, retired, etc.)
- someone displaying similar behavioral elements

Behavioral elements are anything that characterizes how a guest behaves in public and how they expect to be treated. These are different depending on the location and vary depending on psychographic segments. For instance, your parents or your children might have completely unique behavioral elements from you.

These are some of the main behavioral elements of guests:

- Emotional and social distance. *They may not want to be hugged or asked about their personal struggles when you first meet them.*

- Distrust of the church. *They may struggle to connect church and authenticity, or they may think the church just wants their money.*
- Desire to be in control. *They may need to initiate contact, and you should allow them that privilege. The church normally prefers to initiate, so this may feel out of the norm. Serve the environment and the person, but go slow and let the guest be in control.*
- Expect people to be responsive. *They may want your guest services team to be timely and helpful and to embrace responsibility throughout the process.*

If you're a leader, you should train and staff your team using this type of psychographic information. Let your team know what to expect. Introduce them to the guest and teach them to empathize with what they might experience during a visit.

Properly using psychographic information can make a large church feel small in the best ways, and a small church feel large in the best ways. Imagine this scenario: A guest wants to get involved in a marriage group. They approach a greeter. The volunteer gives them a ten-second answer but also collects their contact information. "I'd also like to send you an email right now with some more information that you can review at your leisure. Don't worry, you won't be added to our mailing lists. We're emailing you one time." (Request only an email address, because a phone number and address feels too invasive.) When the guest opens their inbox, they find a brief, helpful email that says, "If we can be more helpful, please email _____." This puts control back into the guest's hands.

This can make a small church feel large, because the system is responsive and not too invasive. It can also make a large church feel small, because you got back to them quickly, remembered who they are, and gave them a personal point of contact.

Getting the Whole Team There

So we've presented the goal, but how do you get there with your team?

You don't need to use the term *psychographics*. But your team should create an outline of what your typical guest looks like. Even though you'll experience diversity at your church, you'll notice a trend toward a certain type of person your church naturally reaches. Create a sheet that outlines the values, preferences, and life stage of that person. Get specific—down to things like shows they watch, magazines they read, and life goals they have. Check out the appendix for an example of a psychographics sheet. Narrow down the focus of your hospitality team by introducing them to the guest. Tell them, "This is the person we have coming through our door. How should we respond to them?"

A great way to start integrating a welcoming atmosphere for this type of guest is through inviting new people to become part of the team. Invite people to your team who reflect the guest. Look for people with the right body language, a responsive nature, and even a style that reflects your target guest's psychographic state.

If you're the leader of the team, train your current team to start empathizing with the guest. Note: a new approach can take a long time for them to get right. Be patient with this. Listen and continue to reinforce the vision and the why behind this new approach.

Some people might not see it. But that's okay, as long as you can get people to *feel* it. For good or for bad, so much of guest services is driven by emotion. So give your team of volunteers an emotional landscape they can relate to.

Start by using the word *imagine*. Imagine if . . .

- a guest saw themselves in the way you responded to them.
- a guest felt comfortable in our ministry, even though they've harbored distrust for religion.
- a guest felt so at ease in the church that they could focus completely on the worship and message.
- a guest felt in control of the situation, even when they've been completely out of control the rest of the day.

Once they have imagined the scenario, close with some questions: "What if we could make a guest feel like that? What is it going to take for us to do that?" Guide them to the right answers.

Continue to lead your team with vision as they adjust to the new approach to knowing the guest. It takes thirty days to navigate and learn a new habit, so you'll need patience as you see your team reinforce and adopt this new behavior as part of their hospitality culture.

Change doesn't have to be sudden. In fact, your best opportunity to get your ministry to know your guest will be small changes over a period of time. Imagine if, each week, you made small changes to better reach your guest. You make one small tweak, then you evaluate it. The next week, you make another small tweak, then evaluate. Over a year's time, that's fifty-two small changes. While each change might not have been revolutionary, the sum of all those changes at the end of the year would be massive. It helps keep you from having knee-jerk reactions and it helps bring the rest of the team along for the journey.

As these changes happen, some of your current team might become displeased or frustrated with the new system. Give them time. But if a volunteer simply isn't getting on board, you should never sacrifice the comfort of a guest for the preferences of a volunteer. In other words, there may come a point where you need to fire a volunteer.

As a leader, yes, you *can* fire a volunteer. You don't need to be mean about it. You don't need to disgrace them. But if you have given them time to adopt new behaviors and have done all you can to train them, but they still aren't getting it, you need to do something. Meet with them, and see where their passions lie. You might find out they're better suited to work in production. They might be better suited to work with children. Help them find a new post that will relieve both your and their frustration.

Businesses don't have quite the same luxury that churches do; they can't just always shift an underperforming employee to a different part of the organization. Firing, though, is not a bad thing. For some people, getting fired is the best thing that can happen to them. It can set them up to learn how to approach their job better in their next employment situation, and it can help them find the position that's best suited for them. Don't be afraid to let go of people who aren't getting it.

At the end of the day, we are here to create remarkable hospitality for our guest. An inflexible volunteer throws a monkey wrench in the whole thing. Don't allow that to happen. Do all you can, but don't be afraid to lose a volunteer. Protect the guest's experience at all costs.

What about Getting "Too Targeted"?

So often in our ministries, we think we're designing an experience for a guest, but we're really designing it for ourselves. We're designing it for regular attendees like us. Or worse, we are trying to create an experience for everyone, which means we create an experience for no one.

In 1 Corinthians, we see how the early church was already dividing into sects. One group of people was proud to follow Peter. Others to follow Paul. Others, Apollos. And of course there were those "super spiritual" people who only followed Christ. Paul, in his letter to the Corinthians, fought against this: we're all in this together. But at the same time, we can't deny the fact that some people seemed to relate better to Apollos, others to Peter, and others to Paul. In fact, some people straight up didn't like Paul—he was a salty character at times.

Focusing on identifying your guest is quite simply acknowledging the people who will relate best to your pastor and your church. Is your pastor an Apollos? A Peter? A Paul? It's about identifying your guest and creating an experience that will best reach the people you're naturally going to reach. It's not about competition—that's what Paul was fighting against in 1 Corinthians. As much as I wish we could all meet together in a gigantic stadium each weekend, it just isn't possible. So smaller churches spread out across the city is a necessity.

This is actually a good thing. We are all in this together, but churches will reach different types of people.

When you create an avatar of a person—using psychographic data—you leave people out. The purpose isn't to be exclusive but to make it easier to help the right person find the right church quickly. Many people will come in and out of your church. The *periphery* of your target audience won't always stay. But your *target* does stay, along with the people who have a vision for reaching that target. And you create a remarkable experience for those guests when they do arrive.

► JASON

My pastor, Andy Stanley, received an email from one of his staff members that I think paints a perfect picture of what's possible when you know the guest. This man was a former atheist who used to attend church with his wife. He eventually became a Christ follower and is now on staff at North Point Ministries. I'd like to share portions of the letter with you.

> For a long time, attending was about honoring the wishes of my wife. I did it for her. Eventually, it was valuable to me and my intellectual well-being. Back then, I used to skip a lot because the music was excruciating to sit through as well. The quality was amazing, but I could not appreciate the content, and I was very intolerant of standing on my feet through 3–4 songs.

> But what kept me coming back was this: It's like the whole team went out of their way to simultaneously acknowledge Christian stereotypes, and then behave contrary to them. It's like you knew I expected to be bored. You knew I expected the pastor to use cryptic language. You knew I expected to be inundated with religious imagery and tradition. You knew I expected a culture war. You knew I expected an offering plate to be forced through my fingers in front of everyone else.

> You knew I expected to feel awkward and uncomfortable for the duration of my experience, and you intentionally took steps to not fit in the mental box I had created for you.

■ ■ ■

Imagine if your ministry knew the guest so well that this could be said about you. You could see their concerns and know their points of anxiety, then do everything in your power to be different—to pleasantly surprise them by being different than what they feared.

Clint Jenkin, vice president of Barna Research, once told me, "The guest is more concerned with being comfortable than knowing we're glad they're here." Every church is glad that a first-time guest chose to visit. That's nothing remarkable. But not every church is able to make that guest feel comfortable when they are there. And that's what a first-time guest truly values.

Of course, this can feel like consumerism. After all, Jesus didn't die on the cross so we could be comfortable coming to church. But at the same time, that doesn't mean we need to *make* people feel uncomfortable when they enter our parking lots and doorways.

By crafting an atmosphere of empathy, we have the opportunity to experience things like that letter from a former atheist. We can meet our guests where they are, then surprise them because of our knowledge of their expectations. We can provide what they're looking for, then avoid the things they're hoping they don't experience.

Know the guest, and the guest will want to know you. Remember that how you feel about a guest coming in will be reflected in how they feel about you going out. When you know the guest and they feel it, they'll feel valued—you'll get the come back effect. But more than that, it is a step toward them knowing Jesus—all because you took the time to get to know them.

KEY POINTS and TAKEAWAYS

1. Creating the come back effect starts with knowing more about the guest than just census data. You should know the values, attitudes, and interests of your guests.
2. You can get to know your guest better by asking, (a) "What went right?" (b) "What went wrong?" (c) "What was missing?" (d) "What was confusing?"

3. When it comes to relating to and knowing the guest, one or two stories from your guests shouldn't cause you to change everything you do as a ministry. Don't make knee-jerk reactions; instead look for overall trends to indicate what changes you should make.

4. Respond to your guest, but don't be invasive. Knowing your guest's persona well allows the guest to be anonymous when they want while still making the experience feel personal.

5. Fifty-two small changes over the course of a year is more manageable than two or three big changes. Your team will respond best to small tweaks made over time as it relates to knowing and relating with the guest.

6. In your community, some people will relate better to your pastor, church, or ministry than other people will. Having a target audience is simply acknowledging that and helping you reach those people.

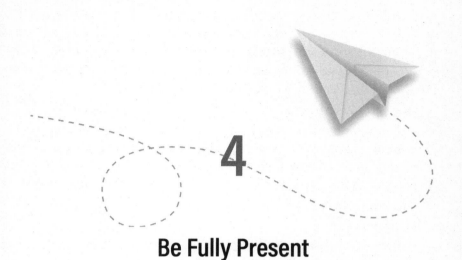

Be Fully Present

▶ JONATHAN

The other day I was working from a local coffee shop that was about half an hour away from my house. I'd finished the workday early—before rush-hour traffic hit—and got in my car to head home.

About thirty minutes after I closed the door to my car, I pulled into my parking spot at the apartment complex and turned off the engine. It's like I emerged from an unconscious state as I realized I had no idea how I'd gotten home.

I couldn't remember what route I took. I couldn't remember if I'd experienced road rage along the journey. I didn't even know what music was playing while I navigated the city streets. Throughout the whole journey, I was so lost in my own thoughts that I didn't process any external stimuli. I was completely inside my own head.

■ ■ ■

Surely you can relate to that experience. We've all been through situations where our internal autopilot kicks in, and we skate through life completely unaware of what we're doing.

It's even easy to do this in our ministries. When each week looks and feels like more of the same, it's easy for autopilot to kick on inside our heads. We're performing functions and doing our job, but our minds are wandering around elsewhere. We aren't in the moment. If we want excellence in hospitality, we can't afford for anyone on our teams to be like this. We have to be fully present in the moment.

If you're familiar with any psychological or new age teachings, you've probably heard of this concept of being "fully present." It's interchangeable with mindfulness, thoughtfulness, being in the moment . . . It's listening. Awareness. Presence.

There's a story told of Buddha that illustrates being "fully present" perfectly.

One day the Buddha was speaking to a prince who asked him, "What do you and your monks practice every day?"

The Buddha replied, "We sit, we walk and we eat."

The prince said, "We also do these things every day, so how are you different?"

The Buddha responded, "When we sit, we know we are sitting. When we walk, we know we are walking. When we eat, we know we are eating."[1]

Mysticism aside, being fully present is simply being aware of what you're doing. It's about knowing why you're doing what you're doing. In Buddhism, this is because awareness is a transcendental state.

For our purposes, though, being fully present has a completely different motivation. In Buddhism, it's about being self-aware. But in the come back effect, being fully present is about being aware of both yourself *and* the guest. It's about being externally focused, so you can fully empathize and connect with your guest. It's laying aside yourself and giving the guest your everything.

When you make the intentional choice to be fully present, you are declaring what you value. Will you value the restaurant you want to visit once the church service is over? Will you value that text message buzzing in your pocket? Or will you put all those distractions aside and value the guest?

A parent understands this concept. When a big football game or *Dancing with the Stars* is on the television and his or her child is begging for attention, they have a choice. The parent can try to focus on both—attempt to catch their child's antics in between football hikes or dance numbers. Or the parent can mute or turn off the television and focus all their attention on the child—becoming fully present in that moment.

We all know which one of those scenarios is the right response. (Though acting on it is often much more difficult in the moment.) But through the right response, you get a benefit greater than the thrill of entertainment. When we connect with the life of another person, we both get a lift. It's mutually beneficial. The connection a parent has with their child is far greater—at least in the long run—than that TV show (even the Super Bowl).

That's what we're talking about in this chapter. The come back effect is more than just blocking and tackling on the field of your ministry. It's not just coordinating Xs and Os in the game plan. It's about human interaction. When we choose to relate with the guest, we create a great experience.

THE COME BACK EFFECT

The intentional human element turns a potentially impersonal process—shuffling people from their car, through the lobby, to the event, and back out—into a moment when the guest feels valued and heard.

The Four Fields of Operation

When we talk about being fully present, there are four fields of operation on which we must play the game. Being present in one of these, but not the other three, will make for a breakdown in the come back effect. And while it's impossible to analyze your presence in these four fields in the moment, being aware of these areas ahead of time can help you be more fully present for the guest.

Spiritual
► JASON

Anthony and Susan are a newly married couple who serve in guest services. They're navigating what it means to maintain a godly marriage.

David, on the other hand, is the CEO of a major company. He's learning what it means to lead under the extreme pressure of the corporate world while still maintaining a healthy home life that isn't all about his conquests. David will obviously have a different approach to hospitality than Anthony and Susan. And that's true of you and every other member of your team.

■ ■ ■

Each volunteer or staff member will have a different motivation for serving. Anthony and Susan might be learning how serving others and caring for others can make them more empathetic toward each other. David, on the other hand, might just be looking for a chance to give back by assisting others instead of being surrounded by assistants.

Being spiritually "fully present" means understanding what God has entrusted to you and what he's asking of you. It's acknowledging what God is doing in and through you in the role, while also fully focusing on the guest. We need to understand it's a spiritual service—not just a menial task. It's about more than just the role. When your presence meets a deeper understanding of both responsibility and privilege, everything changes.

Never forget the spiritual importance of the come back effect. God has sent people whom he loves to your ministry. He has entrusted their care to you. As the Scriptures tell us in Hebrews 13:2, "Do not forget to show hospitality to strangers, for by so doing some people have shown hospitality to angels without knowing it" (NIV). Showing hospitality to our guests is a very spiritual task.

Businesses aren't excluded from this. You can show the love of Christ through the way you interact with others, even when you're trying to sell them a product or service. Money changing hands doesn't negate the opportunity to demonstrate the kindness of God through your hospitality.

Mental

When a man has a conversation with his wife, being mentally present is about the thinking element of conversation. As his wife begins talking, he presses Pause on what he's thinking and presses Play on what she's saying. A thoughtful husband thinks through appropriate questions to ask that will foster the conversation. He thinks through answers to her questions.

He doesn't just listen to keywords. "I went to the store and the clerk was so mean to me." *Store, clerk,* and *mean* might be the keywords, which communicate the facts of what happened. But wrapped up in a sentence like that is so much more depth. There are emotions and deeper truths about the wife found in the middle of those keywords. She was expecting something different to happen. She felt a deeper pain than just the pain of someone being mean to her. It might have even reminded her of a painful experience as a child, when someone treated her unfairly. A thoughtful husband hears more than just the facts. He listens to the story and then listens through to what his wife is really saying.

That's the start of being mentally "fully present." Stopping our thoughts and fully engaging with the guest. Taking it a step further, though, you should be listening for the deeper question the guest is asking—sometimes even when there's no actual question involved. Instead of answering the question they explicitly ask, take your response to the next level and offer them an answer to what they're really asking but might be afraid to express.

Disney World trains their cast members (they aren't called employees) to do this well. A famous example is drawn from those people who approach a cast member with the question, "What time is the three o'clock parade?" The answer is obvious: 3:00 p.m. But Disney employees hear this question all the time. And they've been trained to realize that people are *actually* saying, "I need to know when I should get to the parade and where I should sit." A well-trained Disney employee will respond with, "There's a great spot to see the parade at _____. If you get there by 2:25 you'll have to sit there waiting for thirty-five minutes, but your kids will love it. They'll get to sit up front and see the characters." You see, the Disney employee answered the verbalized question, but they also answered the *real* question.

► JASON

Another example comes from a time my family and I stayed at the Ritz-Carlton in Atlanta, Georgia. I called the front desk the morning we were to leave the hotel, asking, "What time is check-out?" My real question was, "Will we have time to do what we want before we have to check out of the hotel?" Of course, I was afraid to ask that of the front-desk employee. Fortunately, they heard my *real* question and replied, "Is there a certain time you would like to check out?" I told the employee what we wanted to accomplish, and she replied, "Normal checkout is 11:00 a.m. But how about this: We can set your checkout time to 1:00 p.m. or a little later. That should give plenty of time for you and your family to enjoy yourselves. Would that be helpful?"

■ ■ ■

Did you notice how, in each of those situations, being fully present meant taking excellence to the next level? That isn't an easy thing to do if you're thinking about your own problems while trying to listen to the guest. Providing excellence like that requires that you press Pause on what you're thinking and fully invest your mental energy into the guest.

Let's set up a typical church scenario to see if we can discover what a *real question* might sound like from a guest.

The service is going to begin in five minutes, and it's moderately full. The back few sections are roped off to encourage people to sit closer to the front and feel like they're part of a good crowd dynamic. After all, your church doesn't want anyone to feel like they're sitting alone or that they're too far away from the action of the service. There's still plenty of room in the non-roped areas.

A young mother with a baby approaches an usher, though, and asks if she can sit in the roped-off area. The question seems simple, and policy would dictate "no." But she's actually asking a different question. What she really wants is to sit on the aisle toward the back so she can make a quick exit if her baby starts crying.

If you were listening to the question at face value, you might insist she sit toward the front, in the middle of a row, so she can feel connected with the energy of the service. After all, you want her to have a great experience. But if you were listening to her real question, you'd look for an aisle seat toward the back that wasn't roped off. And if there wasn't one, you'd gladly make an exception for her and move the ropes to create space for her.

That's what listening for the *real question* looks like. That's being fully present mentally. It's thinking deeper than the face value of what the guest is verbalizing and reaching them on a deeper level.

Physical
► JONATHAN

One of the most faithful greeters at my church was a successful businessman who had grown up in a family full of boys. Bobby was a tough character, though he loved people and loved his job as a greeter. Unfortunately, because of his rough background—growing up in Boston with brothers who loved to fight—he displayed some odd physical characteristics when he spoke with guests.

Bobby would jut out his chin and look down his nose at the guest as he spoke with them. It gave the impression that he was ready to fight them. When our team approached Bobby and told him about how that appeared to a guest, he was completely unaware he was doing it. It was unintentional body language that he had learned since he was a child.

It took Bobby many weeks of intentionally being aware of his body language to break himself of the habit. But as he focused on being fully present with the guest—being self-aware in order to make the guest feel more welcomed—he became an even better greeter.

■ ■ ■

There's natural body language we all display in different circumstances. When we feel threatened, we cross our arms to feel protected, we avoid eye contact, we frown . . . When we're glad to be around someone, we smile, we brighten our eyes, we open our arms in welcoming gestures, we make eye contact . . . Those positive body language elements are all signs to the guest that we are listening and happy to be doing it. And while a guest might not be fully aware of it, their subconscious is taking cues from our body language and informing them whether they're in a safe environment.

Princeton researchers have found that it takes about 100 milliseconds to register a first impression—as long as it takes a hummingbird to flap its wings.[2] Be aware of body language as you welcome a guest.

Did you know . . .

- when you point your feet toward the guest, you say, "I am interested in what you are saying"?
- when you smile, you say, "I am happy and friendly"?
- when you properly use your hands, you support the words you are saying?
- when you slouch, you say, "I lack confidence or have low energy"?

- when you cross your arms, you say, "I am uninviting or protective"?
- when you look down, you say, "I am uncomfortable or self-conscious"?
- when you listen with eye contact, you say, "I care about you"?
- when you bite your nails or play with your hair, you say, "I am anxious or uncomfortable"?

Becoming aware of your body language takes time and practice. You might role-play in front of a mirror or video yourself in a training session. But becoming more aware of your physical presence will help you not only in hospitality, but in every aspect of your relational life.

The physical element of the come back effect is understanding how your body and expressions communicate to the guest—either making them feel welcomed and safe or putting them in an environment of hostility and emotional distance.

Emotional

The seven most powerful letters in the English alphabet are E-M-P-A-T-H-Y. One reason people pay to see a counselor is because few people in their own life are willing to listen to them with empathy. Your guests are longing to have someone who will listen to them. Imagine what would happen if we could do that for them in the thirty seconds we interact with them.

Being emotionally fully present means feeling their anxiety when they are lost. It means rejoicing with them when they explain how happy they are to have discovered your church. It means expressing concern for them when they misplaced their keys somewhere on the church property (and leaving your post to help find them).

The come back effect involves understanding the emotion and solving the problem in a manner worthy of the emotion of the moment. The empathy should be real. After all, people know when you're faking empathy.

You've experienced this on a phone call with customer service. "I'm sorry you're experiencing this problem. This is just how our company operates." In that interaction, there was no real empathy—the phone operator was not sorry. They were just reading a script.

Many of us have experienced the positive side of this, though, at a restaurant. "I am so sorry your food was cold when we brought it out. We dropped the ball there; that's unacceptable. I'm going to remove that meal from your ticket. Would you like me to bring you out a fresh plate that will be hot? Or how about dessert?" They listened. They empathized with the frustration. And they offered solutions that would solve the real problem as well as the frustration.

Another element of empathy is understanding the negative feelings your guest experiences in every other area of their life and giving them a break from it. For instance, life is hurried. Imagine if you could create the one unhurried moment in their week—letting them set the pace for their visit. That would ignite a desire to come back next week and experience that again. Or perhaps throughout most of their week, they feel ignored and unvalued. If you could listen and value your guest, it would offer them a break from what they normally experience. Your actions and your words could say, "I see you, I hear you, and I value you."

That's hospitality mixed with empathy. That's the emotional field of operation in the come back effect.

What the Guest Hears

When you are not fully present with the guest, you're saying to them:

- "You are not important."
- "You are more of a task to be handled than a person to care about."
- "You will receive more robotic responses from me than personal ones."

Inversely, when you *are* fully present with the guest in these four fields, they hear:

- **"I recognize you.** You are not invisible to me. I intentionally choose not to look past you, but to care enough to look 'in' you. I acknowledge that you might not want to be seen. However, I will be intuitive enough to sense and respond." Not everyone wants to be treated the same. And being fully present allows you to realize the individuality of a guest and respond in a way that's meaningful to them—whether with a handshake or a nod and a smile.
- **"I am listening to you.** I am choosing to actively listen, which means I restate what you are saying to ensure I listened correctly and so you will know you were heard and I 'got' you." Hearing someone is not the same as listening to someone. When you listen, you listen to more than words—you listen to their feelings, their body language, and what they are *not* saying. This allows you to hear the questions they are *really* asking and respond in a way that's meaningful and appropriate.

- **"I want to validate you.** I will normalize the way you are feeling. What you are feeling is common. I don't want you to feel alone in this." Being a guest in a church for the first time is a scary thing. *You* know the pastor won't be sacrificing chickens, but the guest isn't quite sure. When you acknowledge the fear and anxiety your guest may be experiencing, you allow them to relax a little. You acknowledge what they're feeling and assure them that your church is a safe and comfortable place. (Business owners, it's not just churches that are scary for first-timers. Going to any physical location for the first time can be scary.)

- **"I appreciate you.** I realize you are placing trust in our church. You trust us to take care of your children or to invest in your life with our music, words, and care. I don't take this responsibility lightly."

- **"I am giving you my undivided attention.** My posture is toward you. I am looking at you. I am not preoccupied with anything pertaining to me. Distractions lose. You win. You are my priority."

Put your cell phone away. Delay your chat with your usual social group. And focus 100 percent on the guest. After all, the way you feel about a guest coming in will be directly reflected in how they feel about you when they leave.

Practical Ways to Be Fully Present

We've talked about the importance of being fully present. But what does that actually look like? What are some practical ways you can be fully present or ways you can train your volunteers to do this?

1. Watch your body language.

Do a quick full-body scan as you begin your conversation with a guest. *How is my head positioned? Am I making eye contact? Am I smiling?*

Then work your way down. *Are my arms folded or open? Do I have my hands in my pockets? Am I gesturing appropriately?*

Down to your feet. *Are my feet angled toward the guest? Am I standing too close? Too far away?*

Once you've performed the body scan, focus all your attention back on the guest.

2. Intermittently repeat back what you are hearing them say.

Repeating back what you hear your guest saying might feel silly. But it does two things: First, it helps you verify that you're hearing a guest's concerns and questions accurately. Sometimes what we hear isn't actually what's being said. Second, it assures your guests that you are listening to them. Guests want to be heard and understood.

Repetition might look like this: "So I hear you saying you need a seat on an aisle. Would one toward the front work or do you need one in the back?"

3. Be emotionally intelligent.

Emotional intelligence is about understanding and managing yourself and your relationship with guests. That includes matching your words and actions to each setting. What are your tendencies? How do you manage them? Do you recognize the tone of individuals so you know how to best respond? Is the church a casual environment or a formal environment? Is your posture appropriate for such an environment?

What are the guests like who we are serving? Are your actions appropriate for making these types of guests feel welcomed?

How's the pace of the setting? Are people quickly entering and wanting to get to their seats or are they slowly moving toward their seats? Do they want quick conversations or longer conversations?

4. Understand your role in the big picture.

When you encounter a guest, it's important to realize that they don't know your role. They have no idea that your responsibilities might include opening the front door and handing them a bulletin. They don't realize that you're a "lobby greeter." They simply see you welcoming them. They simply experience your guidance as you help them find the children's environment or the worship center. Your role feels monotonous and automatic.

But imagine if you weren't there to perform that task. The guest would feel lost and would be left to find everything on their own. They might wander around for a few minutes trying to find the restrooms, then the children's rooms, and ultimately arrive late to the service. Your role in the big picture is more important than it seems. A guest has no idea what you do, but when they see what you've done it's important.

5. Personalize the experience.

Pay attention to the guest. Quite simply, that means involving the person, responding to them, and empathizing with what they're feeling—what's important to them. This is about personalizing the experience.

Don't treat every guest the same way. Look for ways you can personalize the welcome to the guest. Take cues from their children or spouse, the clothes they're wearing, or the way they walk. Each person walking through your church door is an individual with unique values, dreams, and goals in life. Look for their individuality and customize the guest experience for them.

6. Accomplish your tasks early.

You shouldn't have to be *working* when a guest arrives. If you're sorting through the bulletins as a guest arrives with a question, you won't be able to be fully present for them. When you're unhurried, you can more easily be undistracted for the guest. You can focus all of your attention—spiritual, mental, physical, and emotional—on the guest.

Imagine your ministry being the one place where a guest feels truly heard. The one place in their life that feels unhurried and peaceful. We have the opportunity to offer empathy and comfort in a world filled with chaos.

When we do what we do best, then God does what he can do best. Something amazing happens when we're fully present for our guests.

KEY POINTS and TAKEAWAYS

1. Great personal hospitality requires being fully present—nothing distracting you from fully engaging with the guest.

2. There are four fields of operation where we have the opportunity to be fully present: spiritual, mental, physical, and emotional. Excellent hospitality in ministry requires relating with the guest on each of those arenas.

3. Here are six practical ways to be fully present:

   a. Watch your body language.

   b. Intermittently repeat back what you are hearing them say.

   c. Be emotionally intelligent.

   d. Understand your role in the big picture.

   e. Personalize the experience.

   f. Accomplish your tasks early.

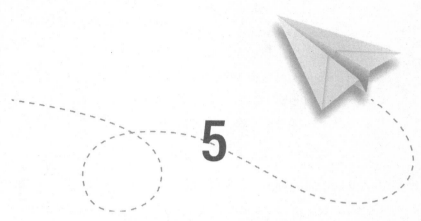

5

Think Scene by Scene

Churches and businesses like to think in terms of functions. We want to know: Who will pass the offering buckets? Who will help people find seats? Who will keep our parking lot from becoming too chaotic? These are all roles that need staffing.

So we look for a team to fill these roles. That gives us a parking lot team to manage traffic, a greeting team to hand out bulletins, and an usher team to seat people and pass the offering buckets. Then in the middle of this, we assign them the task of welcoming people and making them feel comfortable.

Unfortunately, the guest doesn't think like this. They have no idea all the tasks a parking lot attendant performs. They don't know what a greeter does or what roles an usher performs. Instead, the guest thinks in terms of scenes. Their thought process looks something like this:

Scene 1:   The Drive to the Church

Scene 2:   Finding a Parking Spot

Scene 3:   Walking to the Front Doors

Scene 4:   Navigating the Lobby

Scene 5:   Dropping Off the Children

Scene 6:   Entering the Worship Center and Finding a Seat

Scene 7:   Picking Up the Children

Scene 8:   Finding the Car

Scene 9:   Escaping the Parking Lot without Sitting in Traffic

Scene 10: The Drive to a Restaurant

You see, for them, attending your church service is an adventure story akin to *The Lord of the Rings*—especially if it's their first time.

They're on a journey, much like Frodo with his ring. Along the way, there will be inconveniences and stress points. Those along the path will either become allies, obstacles, or enemies. And each new scene they encounter will either be a place of healing or a place of hostility.

What will your ministry be in this story? Will it be Mordor—a place of dangers and stress? Will it be Rivendell—a place of healing?

What will your role be in the story? Will you be an Orc—someone adding stress and anxiety to the situation? Will you be a Sam—someone easing their burden?

Just like *The Lord of the Rings*, each scene of your church is a moment of potential conflict. "Will I be able to find the church and deal with the traffic? Will they have a parking spot for me? Will I find the correct entrance to the church? Will I know where to go once I'm inside the building? Are people going to look at me weird? Is the pastor going to make me do something embarrassing in the middle of the service?"

They don't care if the parking lot team placed the traffic cones in the appropriate lanes. They don't care if the greeter is standing in her assigned space. They certainly don't care if the ushers placed a box of tissues on the back row of each aisle. They are thinking about which rooms and spaces they'll have to visit. If you look at the scene list, that's quite a few spaces. And we didn't even include bathrooms, nursing mothers' rooms, multiple buildings, or first-time guest rooms.

Each of those spaces complicates the process and creates a potential for conflict. Your job in extending hospitality is to ease those points of tension. The crazy thing about it is that some of these scenes are outside of your control. But for the guest, it is still all part of visiting your church.

▶ JASON

At Buckhead Church in Atlanta, Georgia, we've been navigating this idea. We have been trying to decide where our control of the guest experience begins. We understand that several roads feed our location, but there is one major entry point that requires more attention than any other.

When you pull off Highway 400, you turn onto Lenox Road and turn left onto Tower Place Drive. The church is right there, with its 320 parking spaces and three rented parking decks that surround the church. Because vehicles are entering and leaving our parking decks, our control obviously starts on Tower Place Drive. We're creating the traffic chaos, so we need to manage it for our guest. But even more than that, our control begins on Lenox Road—at the long red light that awaits our guest. Obviously, we can't do much about the length of the light other than staff it with highway patrol who can direct traffic, but we're constantly looking for ways we can help the guest navigate that scene of their journey.

The next scene? Looking for a parking spot. Again, we can't control the other drivers in our decks, but we do our best to ease the tension of this scene through our parking team.

During every incremental scene, it's important to ask, "What is the guest thinking and feeling?" Then we do our best to anticipate their needs in each scene.

One simple way we have anticipated needs is understanding that if you are a parent with an infant or a preschool-age child, you carry other items with you. Therefore, we want to make the walk as easy as possible for you and provide a shorter distance for you to walk. You will see street signs that tell you to put your flashers on and we will guide you to park in the deck underneath the church. There we have an express elevator for you to get to your child's ministry environment. At some of our campuses, we even provide wagons in the parking lots, creating a fun way to tote preschoolers and all of the accessories that go along with parenting that age group.

■ ■ ■

Breaking Down the Scenes

What are the different scenes in your ministry? Where does one scene stop and another scene start? For each organization, the breakdown of the scenes will be different.

The natural place to start is with location. Go to Google Maps and grab an aerial shot of your building or draw a diagram of your area. Walk through the process of a guest who is choosing to visit. (Use your demographic/psychographic information to inform you of what your guest will need to do while there—their family, their age, and so forth.) What happens when they first pull into the parking lot? Then what happens when they walk to the front door?

The first part of this scene-by-scene process is naturally your parking area and building. Your rooms, doors, and hallways will determine what different scenes your guest encounters. If your ministry is blessed with good architecture, this might not be a challenge for your guest. But if the layout of the building and the rooms is confusing, this becomes an obstacle. What will you do to help people overcome these obstacles and get to the next scene?

The second part is what you create. For instance, by putting volunteers in certain locations, you might actually be placing a barrier in the guest's mind. Some people don't want to have to talk to someone or shake someone's hand on their way to the restrooms. Some people don't want to deal with a gauntlet of greeters before they find the safety of their seat. Structures we create might be the very thing adding difficulty to the story.

The third part of the scene-by-scene process is what the guest assumes. Depending on their background, they'll naturally imagine certain scenes based on their past experiences. Those might either be things they're looking forward to or things they're dreading (like a smile or a grumpy face). They might be sensitive to certain verbiage. Or they might be waiting to be guilted into giving money in the offering plate.

Breaking down the scenes in your guest's experience helps you see where there are gaps in their visit. It helps you identify moments of decision or conflict. (And there *are* moments of decision and conflict in each scene, whether you identify them or not.)

What if, instead of a moment of conflict, you could re-create something about the way the guest thinks, feels, and assumes? For instance, a moment of conflict might be finding a place to sit. But that conflict might be more complex than that. What if the guest needs a place to sit near an aisle, knowing their little one in the nursery might need them midway through the service? How can you re-create your seating situation to easily accommodate a guest with these needs?

What if you could meet your guest on their plane of thought—physically, emotionally, and spiritually? For instance, a guest will be in a different emotional and spiritual state after a more serious altar call than they would if the service ended on a celebratory note. What changes might you need to make to a scene to respond to that?

What if you could make a scene memorable? For instance, can you think of an opportunity to create a moment that surprises and delights your guest? Let's explore this idea of "surprise and delight" a little further.

Surprise and Delight

There's a fine balance between predictability and surprise. People like predictability because it's safe—especially in the context of a church. There's a lot of baggage people have with religion and bad church experiences. They've experienced moments of humiliation or shame. They've experienced things they don't understand that can make them feel uncomfortable.

So when we talk about creating moments of surprise and delight in the scenes at churches, we're talking about moments that don't bring a disruption to the guest's comfort level. For instance, it could be something simple like a fun, tasteful musical opener or an interesting video. Or it could be something like providing popsicles, lemonade, or Kool-Aid in the lobby during a summer sermon series. It's about doing something people didn't see coming, while still fitting within a framework of comfort.

Businesses do this all the time with little extras: free dessert if it's your birthday, bonus room upgrades at a hotel, or packing a little toy or sticker in the shipped package. It's in those extras that you have the opportunity to surprise and delight.

▶ JASON

During baseball season, we served Cracker Jacks and glass Coke bottles from old-school concession "hawker boxes." We made the lobby feel like our attendees were at the big game. We didn't do this at all of our services, but it worked perfectly for the different type of crowd we have at our Sunday evening service.

One of our attendees approached me after the service and said, "Jason, y'all think of everything."

I looked at him and said, "No. We just think of you." (Cheesy, I know.)

These types of things are low-hanging fruit to make your guest's experience excellent. They're easy ways to make a scene memorable.

But an even bigger moment was a story that happened at one of our locations. A couple walked in and asked where they could get some coffee. They assumed because we are a large church that we have a coffee shop. We don't at any of our locations. One of our volunteers replied, "We don't have a coffee shop. But I tell you what. Between you and me . . . Follow me. I want to take care of you." He took them to the guest services room and served them a cup of coffee from the volunteer refreshments. Then he escorted them to their seats.

In that moment, our volunteer did something big. He turned a potential disappointment into a moment of surprise and delight.

■ ■ ■

It's in those "no" situations that you will most often find the opportunity to create a moment of surprise and delight for a guest. When you can work around a restrictive policy and make the guest feel uniquely valued, you have created a "wow" in the guest's mind. That's memorable.

Transitioning Scenes

One part of great storytelling is creating great scenes. But the story becomes choppy if the storyteller doesn't easily transition between the scenes. Your goal in hospitality is to help your guests transition seamlessly between the various scenes they'll encounter.

It's obvious when an organization doesn't think through this scene-transition element. You've probably dealt with this on a support call to a company. When you call to make a purchase, you get the A-level phone bank workers. They're quick and responsive to every request you have. But then, when you call back in a week or so to report a problem, the phone bank worker says they can't help you. "You'll need to talk to our support staff." Then they give you a phone number to call their outsourced support branch in a foreign country. You call, then have to restate your problem. The customer support employees do their best to be helpful, but ultimately there isn't much they can do to help. The transition between your first scene (purchasing the product) and your next scene (product support) was choppy.

You see, the customer doesn't think in terms of roles. They don't think about the difference between sales and support staff.

They just want help. But since the company hasn't done a good job at working out the transitions between scenes, they've created a bad experience for the customer. They've forced them to have to adapt to the organization's system instead of the system adapting to the customer.

Imagine if you called a company's support line and got help from the first person who took your call. Sure, they might have to say, "Let me get in touch with our support staff and get that fixed for you. Can I put you on a brief hold?" But you'd gladly hold on the line, knowing someone's taking care of the problem without you having to jump through organizational hoops.

Now imagine this idea of transitioning scenes applied to your ministry. What would it look like to create a seamless end-to-end experience?

1. A guest pulls into the parking lot and a parking attendant guides them to the closest available spot: the spot that's most obvious to the guest . . . not the spot that's most convenient for the parking attendant's system.

2. The guest exits their car and sees a sign over the entrance making it clear where they need to go next. They don't have to guess where the main entrance is.

3. The guest enters the lobby and a greeter notices their children. "We have great age-appropriate kids' activities planned this morning. Would you like me to escort you and your children to our children's ministry?" The guest services volunteer doesn't make the guest ask where to go. But they also don't force the guest to ship their kids off to a figurative boarding school.

4. The guest services volunteer walks the guest through the check-in process by linking up with a specialist in the kids'

environment instead of just dropping them off with kids' volunteers.

5. After the kids are checked in, the guest services volunteer reassures the family that their children will have a great time and offers to escort the family to the auditorium.

6. The guest services volunteer helps the family find a great seat, then informs them, "I'll be right outside in the lobby where you first met me if you need anything else."

In the above scenario, there isn't a point where the guest even needs to ask a question. The team members and the signage anticipated what the guest would need in each scene and helped them transition seamlessly between scenes. And while it might not be feasible for your team to function like that completely, the principle still applies. The goal is to keep the guest from even having to ask the obvious questions. Sure, there will always be random questions that are impossible to anticipate. But when you are quick enough to provide the answers you *can* anticipate, the guest will feel comfortable asking the ones you *can't*.

It's important to note that the goal is not to shuffle people through the scenes as fast as possible. Hospitality is a process, but you shouldn't make your guest *feel* processed.

▶ JONATHAN

Have you ever been through the ordering line at Chipotle? They're masters at processing through customers. They ask you questions before you've even had the chance to make a request. (White rice or brown? Black beans or pinto beans? What kind of meat do you want?) It's even a fun game I've played once or twice—trying to state my order before they've had the chance to ask. I've never succeeded in beating them to the punch. They're good. And while that works great for a fast-food restaurant, it doesn't work so well for a ministry.

■ ■ ■

You want to make transitioning scenes a simple process, but you don't want to rush people through the procedure. Put the power in the guest's hands. Let them progress through as slowly or as quickly as they like. Remember, if you're new to a place, it takes awhile to take everything in. Let them absorb the sights and sounds without rushing them through the activity.

Whose Story Is It Anyway?

Each time we meet in our churches, we're telling a story to our guest. It will either be an exciting story with a happy ending, or it'll be a tragedy that leaves our guests unwilling to return the next week. Obviously we want to tell a good story. And while our message might be the greatest story ever told—the story of Jesus—the story of our hospitality is about someone else.

One of the greatest perspective shifts we can make in hospitality is understanding who the hero of the story actually is. As a volunteer or staff member, we find it natural to put ourselves in that hero role. We want to be the protagonist of the story. But if we're going to be truly excellent at hospitality, we have to take a supporting role. The true hero of the story is the guest. Their visit to the church is *their* story.

The question we have to ask ourselves is this: Will we be a villain in the story? An inconvenient obstacle? Or an ally?

There will be plenty of villains in their story, like the guy who runs the red light on their drive to church. There will be inconvenient obstacles, like their kids who can't seem to find their shoes. Your guest doesn't need any more villains or obstacles in their story. The come back effect is choosing to be the ally in the guest's story.

Don't just greet your guest. Be their ally. Or if you aren't the person to do that, connect them with the right people. Introduce them to the friend who will help them get where they need to go.

They need an ally. They need someone who will help them overcome these obstacles. They need someone they can rely on who will help them reach the happy ending of their story.

It's too easy to think about our own story. We get lost in our own obstacles and our own villains. "Are we going to run out of coffee? Is my breath bad? Did Tom ever show up for his volunteer position, or am I going to have to do his job too?" While these obstacles do matter, we can't afford to think about our story when it's time to welcome guests. We have to be fully focused on helping them tell *their* story.

Is your hospitality set up in such a way that the hero of your story can get from scene to scene without a massive battle or crisis? Is your team positioned in such a way that a guest will feel comfortable asking for help—no matter how intimidating that request might be?

▶ JASON

Fred is a greeter who understands this idea. He's a young grandfather type who gets the concept of making other people the hero of the story. He gets on his hands and knees all the time and high-fives kids. He's not weird about it; he just loves people. And he's so authentic about it that young families absolutely love him.

A woman came up to him with her son recently and said, "Excuse me, sir. You look like the type of man that would pray for us." Fred gladly stepped away from the door and was fully present with her and her son as he prayed for them.

After the prayer, the woman confided in Fred. "My son is twelve years old. He celebrates his thirteenth birthday today. He doesn't know yet, but we found out that his dad only has a couple of weeks left to live. And I have to tell him this on the week of his thirteenth birthday. I just looked at you and knew you would pray for us."

If Fred had been consumed with his own story instead of passionate about the guest's, this lady would have probably walked right past him and looked for someone else. But because Fred was fully present and made this lady the hero of the story, he was able to offer hope and encouragement to her—even if only for a few minutes.

■ ■ ■

When you get lost in your role, you miss out on opportunities like this. A guest doesn't care about your role. They don't care if you are there to seat them or help them find a parking spot. They really just want to know that you're there for them. Guests pay attention to who you are. Not what you do.

Ask yourself this question: Do you look like the type of person who people would think could pray for them? Is the guest the hero in your eyes?

At each scene in your ministry, does the guest feel like they belong? Do they feel like you've done the difficult work of creating scenes that make it easy for them to get where they need to go? Will they want to come back—to relive this story week after week?

KEY POINTS and TAKEAWAYS

1. Guests don't think in terms of tasks or roles; they think in terms of scenes and barriers to where they want to go. One of your most important jobs in hospitality is to remove those barriers.

2. The primary barriers your guests will experience are based on the physical location and arrangement of your building, your own organizational structure and red tape, and your guests' assumptions about what they will experience.

3. Make the experience of a guest's visit safe and predictable. However, when it doesn't negatively affect the guest's comfort level, add moments of surprise and delight.

4. A guest's experience should feel seamless—not departmental and choppy. Make the handoff between your ministry's roles feel like one big experience instead of many small ones.

5. Your guest is the hero in the story of their visit; your role is the ally.

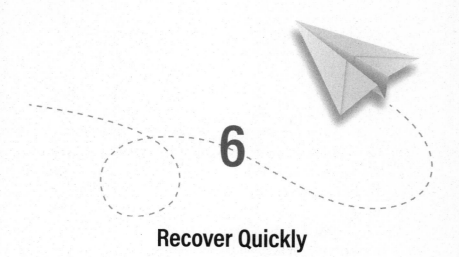

6

Recover Quickly

► JASON

Our churches close the doors to the auditorium when we have baptisms. We show a brief video story of the person getting baptized before each baptism, and we've found that when the doors are opened during a video, guests still want to be seated, and light streams into the room. Both distract people from the moment. So we position greeters at the doors while the videos play to let people know what's going on. They guide them to the monitors in the lobby so they can still take part in the service and know when it's time to go back into the auditorium.

At one of our locations one day, the doors were closed for baptisms. A young mother with a two-year-old child approached the auditorium doors wanting to get inside. One of our guest services volunteers, Jane, met her at the door, and I watched from a distance as she explained why we keep the doors closed. I assumed everything would proceed normally, but I saw the young mother get visibly frustrated. She walked away to the couches and sat down, obviously unhappy.

Jane approached me with a nervous face. She knew she had made a mistake. She explained, "Here's what happened. I informed this lady that we kept the doors closed to limit distractions. Apparently, her sister was the one being baptized at that moment. I told her it was our policy that we keep the doors closed, so she couldn't go in. I realize now that I should have just let her in. She's really unhappy. What should I do now, Jason?" Jane's a by-the-books team member, but even she realized she should have bent the rules this time. A conversation should have trumped a standard policy.

I suggested she go to the young mother and apologize to her. But when Jane tried to apologize, you could tell it was too late. The damage was done and the young mother wanted nothing to do with Jane. There was a very real, very personal offense that had taken place.

That's when Roger stepped into the picture. Roger is amazing at providing customer service at the insurance agency he owns. He eats, sleeps, and breathes guest services.

Roger saw the situation and told me, "Jason, I have an idea. I'll be right back."

He walked out of the church building and returned around fifteen minutes later. He walked up to me and handed me four Starbucks gift cards. "I know problems are going to happen again at some point in the future. Hang on to these and give them to people when something goes wrong." Then he walked up to the young mother with one of the gift cards.

As Roger spoke with her, I saw her whole demeanor change. Roger's presence changed the situation for her. He said, "Ma'am,

I'm so sorry. What happened a few minutes ago was absolutely our fault. We messed up, and we apologize. You deserved to be in that auditorium, but we said no. I'm sorry." Her whole disposition changed as he spoke.

He continued, "I know this doesn't fix the situation, but I wanted to give you this Starbucks gift card. Maybe you can use it for a little break from parenting or to meet up with your sister."

She responded, "You don't have to do that." The situation was already resolved by that point.

But Roger replied, "You're right. We don't have to do that. But we want to make things right and apologize." Roger stayed with the young mother and kept talking, interacting with her and her young child.

I watched this unfold from a distance and couldn't help but smile. Roger recovered quickly and made things right. His presence changed her disposition, his empathy changed everything, and he owned the situation. Even though he didn't cause the problem, he took ownership.

■ ■ ■

Here's the thing: Even in the midst of serving people well, things can go wrong. People get their feelings hurt or we fail to meet their expectations. And it's up to us to make things right. The come back effect is about recovering, and recovering quickly.

Why do we focus on recovering quickly? Is it to make the guest feel better? Yes, but that's a by-product. For Christ followers, recovery is about demonstrating the kindness of God. In our ministries, we lead people into a growing relationship with God. Elevating the dignity of the guest helps people see the kindness of God through our actions and ultimately leads them back to him. It's the kindness of God that leads people to repentance (Rom. 2:4). We are Christ's ambassadors, given that same ministry of reconciliation (2 Cor. 5:18). Our kindness is the extension of God's kindness.

If you're simply trying to make the guest feel good, you're providing customer service. But the church is called to more than that. (Business leader, you're called to more than that too.) Jesus's grace shouldn't become an excuse to be lazy when it comes to showing love to our guests. Instead, it should be our inspiration to do even more.

Things happen. What will we do to make them right?

Preparing for Recovery

There are three major truths when it comes to hospitality in your ministry:

1. Something will go wrong.
2. You aren't perfect (even though you're striving for it).
3. The guest is not perfect.

While those three truths might read negatively, acknowledging them isn't being pessimistic. In ministry and in business, we hope for the best, but we also prepare for the worst. No matter how flawless our hospitality systems and volunteers are, things go wrong. Understanding this helps us put plans into place and prepare to recover.

For instance, you know kids will be coming into your lobby and into your services. Even if you have a great children's program and the kids are supposed to be in their respective rooms, the guest is not perfect. Some guests will choose to keep their children with them in the service despite your suggestions. What happens when the parent has to leave the service because the music was too loud and the child is crying?

You could tell the parent, "I told you so." (And create yet another problem.) Or you could have a plan in place to help the crying child and the distraught parent. Maybe you could have some coloring books in the lobby to help keep the child's mind off the music. Maybe there's an option you can create where the parent can still enjoy the service with less volume.

Or perhaps you recently changed service times at your church. You hope you changed all the service times on social media and the website. You hope you've communicated clearly enough to your church that the service times are changing. But you know some people will have missed the memo. Either you missed one spot on the website or your guests planned their visit before the information had been changed. What do you do when someone shows up in the middle of the service, embarrassed that they got the service time wrong?

Was it your fault? The guest's? It doesn't matter. What matters is what you do to make the guest—who's feeling inconvenienced and embarrassed—feel comfortable once again. Will you ask the guest to come back in an hour when the next service starts (if there's even another service starting)? Will you have a comfortable waiting place where they can watch the rest of the service? Will you escort the guest through a discreet door to a convenient seat near the back where they can at least enjoy the rest of the service?

Preparing to recover is about acknowledging things will happen, and doing your best to quickly make things right. What can you do to prepare for the worst?

The first step in preparing for the worst is knowing the three areas where something can go wrong:

1. With a team member
2. With a guest
3. With the process

A team member or staff member might accidentally offend the guest. The guest might simply be having a bad day. Or there might be a restrictive rule that causes the guest unwanted inconvenience.

Every problem from which you'll need to recover comes from one or a combination of those three things. If you don't know those things, you can't set up something proactive to deal with a problem that arises.

Put a plan into action with your team. Give them some of the tools toward the end of this chapter to help them deal with the emotions of the situation. Give them gift cards or some options to work with when something happens so they can do their best at making restitution. Sometimes, the best preparation you can have is to simply know something might happen so you can prepare yourself emotionally for the event. You know things will go wrong, so prepare yourself and your team for the potential.

It's important to note that even though there are three areas where something can go wrong, we can do something about only two of them. We can fix the team member or we can fix the process. But we can't necessarily fix the guest. One of the big mistakes people make in customer service, though, is to try to fix the customer.

▶ JONATHAN

One of the worst guest experiences I've ever had was at a gymnastics school. The owner failed at recovery—miserably. My wife and I had purchased a summer program for her thirteen-year-old sister. She was staying with us for the summer, and we didn't want her bored at home while we were at work.

We found out after the first day, though, that the summer program was geared more toward children under the age of nine. The program mostly involved coloring and watching the Disney Channel, with only a few minutes of basic gymnastics activities during the day.

So instead of dropping off my sister-in-law the next day, I stayed with her until the owner showed up so I could talk with her. I wanted to see if there was some way I could at least get a partial refund since she did attend the camp for one day.

When the owner finally arrived, I approached the situation as calmly as possible. Having read *How to Win Friends and Influence People*, I put on my best Dale Carnegie charm and told her I thought the program might be a bit age inappropriate for my sister-in-law. "I don't expect to get a full refund for what we paid, but I was wondering if I could at least get a refund for the rest of the days."

The owner had apparently never read *How to Win Friends and Influence People*, because she didn't get what I was trying to do. And she *certainly* didn't respond in a way that made me want to be her friend. Her body language was one of annoyance. And she responded in kind. "I don't know if you can get a refund. I'll have to look at it."

She doesn't know? "Okay . . . So should I leave my sister-in-law here? We did pay for it, so I don't want to waste the money if we can't get a refund."

"I can't tell you that, sir."

"Okay . . . Well, can you at least let me know when you'll know whether or not I can get a refund? I'm just trying to plan my day and figure out what to do here. I don't mean to cause you undue trouble."

"Sir, I told you I can't tell you. I've already told you, and as the owner of this establishment, I have the right to remove you from these premises."

Whoa, that escalated quickly. The situation devolved from there. I'm ashamed to say I lost a bit of my rationality and left the encounter physically trembling with anger.

The owner of this company was trying to recover by changing me. I had a problem first with the process, but she wasn't willing to change that. Then I had a problem with a team member (her), but she wasn't willing to change that either. She was trying to fix me, and that wasn't an option.

■ ■ ■

You can't fix a customer. You can't fix your guest. They are the focal point, not the problem. You can only do your best to fix other things in order to recover.

That story was obviously an example of how *not* to make something right. So how do you go about recovering the right way?

How to Make It Right

There are two types of situations you'll encounter when it comes to recovering with a guest. The first is a reasonable guest who has a justifiable complaint because something went wrong. The faster you resolve these situations, the less emotions will fly around. The second situation is someone whose anger has turned irrational; they have let their emotions go beyond the point of logic. At that point, there's no easy solution. They're looking to rage against the situation.

You aren't likely to fix the situation if it's devolved into irrationality—like the second scenario. In the next section, we'll talk about some strategies for dealing with irrational guests. But for now, we'll talk about the first situation, because that situation can actually be made right.

The first step to making something right when a guest has a complaint is to deal with the feelings first, then deal with the problem second. We talked about this in an earlier chapter. Once a situation arises in which there needs to be recovery, the guest has already begun experiencing the feelings we don't want them to. It becomes an emotional issue instead of just a logical one. And you can't hope to deal with the logic until the emotions have been pacified.

After you acknowledge and address the emotions, then you can start to deal with the situation. Sometimes that might mean someone else needs to deal with the situation—like the story of Jane and the young mother—because the guest associates the emotion with the person. Regardless of who approaches the situation to resolve it, there are seven steps to making things right. These seven steps apply to most situations and can ensure a level of excellence in your ministry for guests.

1. Listen

When someone has a complaint, they've often spent a significant amount of time rehearsing in their head what they plan to say. Let them say it. Let them get it all out. Otherwise you're short-circuiting what they've been rehearsing, and you leave the emotion inside them.

Pardon the gross analogy, but their complaint is like a substance inside of them that needs to get out. They need to vomit it, in a sense. And if you don't let them get it all out, it just sits inside of them and continues to make them sick. Fully hear them out before you continue. Let your listening ear be a healing touch to the emotions inside of them. Once the emotion is out, then you can start working on the solution.

2. Review

One of the best ways to show someone that you're listening is to repeat back to them what they've said. Voice their concerns in your own words so you can guarantee you are both on the same page. Don't patronize them; seek to truly understand.

3. Empathize

Listen first, then feel. You don't have a right to craft a response until the guest is done airing their grievance. Then, empathize before you respond. If you were honest, you'd probably feel the same way they did if you were in their shoes. Feel the emotion they feel.

Often, the situation is fully resolved here. Sometimes empathy is all the guest wants. For some, the emotions are the full extent of the problems. And knowing they are affirmed in what they feel goes a long way.

4. Apologize

Take responsibility even if you don't feel responsible. Even if someone else caused the problem or even if you feel the guest is unjustified in their emotions, apologize. And don't try to get clever with your response by saying something like, "I'm sorry you got offended by this." That shifts the blame back onto the guest for feeling the way they feel instead of taking responsibility for it. People can sense when you aren't being genuine.

5. Resolve

Often, restitution isn't perfect. For instance, it was impossible for Roger to give that young mother a chance to see her sister get baptized in person. Once the offense happened, there was no way to undo the offense. However, he did his best to resolve it some other way.

One of the most empowering things you can do for a guest who feels wronged is to offer them options for restitution. "We want to make this right. We could do _____ or _____. Which would you prefer?" This makes the resolution feel more customized for the guest. (Of course, this means a volunteer needs to be armed with any options that are on the table.)

6. Follow Up

It's important to care in the moment. But if you want to take it to the next level, care after the fact. Follow up with the guest by giving them a call or finding them after the service. People don't necessarily expect follow-up after their problems are resolved, but it's great when it happens.

Make sure this doesn't come from a self-serving motivation. For instance, some car dealerships are great at following up after they've performed service on your car. The call comes in: "We just wanted to make sure you were happy with the service you received. You are? Good! Well, you might receive a call in a couple of days with a survey asking how we did. We'd love it if you rated us five stars across the board."

Those last two sentences ruined the follow-up. It took what was a nice, caring act and turned it into a self-serving act.

7. Discuss

Turn this recovery into a learning opportunity. Write down what happened, then review it with your team in a meeting or an email. This will help you refine your process and prepare for future times when this sort of recovery might be necessary. If you

107

can learn something from one person who had a bad experience, next week you can proactively prepare so somebody else doesn't have the same experience.

Follow those seven steps and you'll have the best chance at turning a bad situation into a positive experience. If you're doing it right, you should never hear these words coming out of your mouth:

- "Calm down." This sort of statement is demeaning.
- "That's not my problem." It's important to take ownership.
- "You're being irrational." If they weren't already irrational, this statement will make them be.
- "What's your problem?" If you ask this, you just made yourself their problem.
- "That's against our policy." This shows the guest that policy takes precedence over them.
- "I'll try to do that." This answer feels noncommittal, like you'll try if you remember to try.
- "Let me know if you have any other problems." This implies the guest will likely have more problems. If the guest knows you handled their problem well, they will come back to you. Instead, maybe say, "Let me know if there's any other way I can help."
- "I don't know." Neither do they. It's your job to figure it out.

If you say any of the things above, you'll probably turn your guest into an irrational guest. Instead, you should hear yourself say:

- "I can see how you feel [insert emotion]."
- "I can imagine that is [insert emotion]."

- "How may I help you today?"
- "I can help."
- "Thank you for letting me help take care of you today."
- "I don't know the answer, but I want to and will find out for you."
- "I am sorry." (With no "but" added.)
- "What I can do for you right now is _____."

Recovering well from a bad situation can be one of the most challenging parts of a ministry of hospitality. But if it's done right, it can turn a bad situation into an excellent one. It's when things go wrong that there's the greatest opportunity to forge a meaningful and memorable connection.

Often the best relationships are forged through adversity. When an individual is willing to humble themselves and make things right, that's when people open their hearts to you. Even though you might have dropped the ball, making things right will turn your guest into a super fan.

- "I love this youth group because they genuinely care about me."
- "I love my small group leader because he actually listens to me."
- "This church doesn't just care about my money. I'm not another number to them. I feel like I have a genuine place I can call home."

Irrational Guests

Finally, how do you deal with a guest who crosses the point of no return? When there seems to be no hope for the situation, how do you respond?

109

First, it's important to acknowledge your own feelings. You have feelings. They are real. If someone's yelling at you, you're probably going to feel like the brown stuff on the bottom of a shoe. But at the same time, you can't let your own feelings interfere with what's going on right now.

You aren't just a tool of the organization. Obviously someone expressing their anger will affect your mood. But you also have a responsibility to rise above what you're feeling and provide hospitality to the guest.

Holly Stiel, in *The Art and Science of the Hotel Concierge*,[1] offers nine tips for helping an angry guest:

1. **"Remain calm and patient."** Proverbs 15:1 tells us, "A gentle answer deflects anger, but harsh words make tempers flare." If you allow your words to become too intense, you're simply adding gasoline to the fire of what they're feeling. Be gentle in your response.

2. **"Feel confident."** Sometimes people fear an irrational guest. Maybe you don't think there's any hope for this type of person. But you were trusted with this role. Don't fear contact with this type of person. You can do it.

3. **"Don't become defensive or intimidated."** Don't let someone intimidate you in your role. You have authority in this situation, even though a yelling guest might make you feel otherwise. You don't have to defend yourself. You don't have to yell. And you certainly don't have to shrink back. True authority removes the need to be defensive.

4. **"Never be condescending to a guest."** Your guest was made in the image of God. They have true value. But when you condescend to a guest, you strip away that value. Let your

body language, tone, and even what you *don't* say reinforce their value in the eyes of God and the eyes of your ministry.

5. **"Avoid offering excuses."** People don't necessarily care why something happened—especially when they've gotten to this point. Logic never fixes feelings, so don't offer excuses. Own the situation.

6. **"Don't blame other departments or individuals for the problem."** People don't care who was at fault. But more than that, if you blame other ministries or individuals, you show disloyalty. It's a form of contempt for the ministry when you point fingers.

7. **"It's never appropriate to argue with a guest."** Arguments don't add anything positive to the experience. The only reason people feel the need to argue is because of a desire for self-preservation or because they want to be right. It's an ego thing. And if this is about your ego, you're not doing hospitality; you're serving yourself. You might consider moving to a more comfortable and personal location, away from the stress of people looking on, and connect in a casual way instead of a formal one.

8. **"Avoid asking too many questions until the guest has had an opportunity to vent."** People need to get out the emotion before they can process the logic of the situation. Don't chime in too fast. Just listen. Let the guest take control of the conversation until they're ready to turn over control to you. This might mean sitting and listening even when everything inside you wants to hurry along the conversation. But the best thing you can do in this situation is let the guest vent.

9. **"Remember: It's not about you."** Don't take it personally. The guest is not really attacking you, as much as it might feel

like it. Even when the guest uses words that feel completely *ad hominem*—words like "you guys" or "you"—the situation is not about you. It's about what the guest feels. Remove yourself from the equation and deal with the situation.

Recovery is one of the hardest parts of the come back effect. It's emotionally draining and uncomfortable. But the biggest "wows" you will ever get—the most memorable moments guests will have with your ministry—will come from properly dealing with these sorts of problems that arise.

God is in the business of redeeming the bad and turning it into something good. In the same way, we have the opportunity to create an amazing experience for a guest even when it all seems to hit the fan.

KEY POINTS and TAKEAWAYS

1. There will be times when you unintentionally ruin an experience for a guest. Acknowledge that it will happen and prepare for it.
2. You aren't perfect and the guest isn't perfect either, but you can only control the first part. You can't control the guest.
3. Knowing a breakdown in hospitality will occur, give your team tools to help make things right when something does go wrong.
4. When something goes wrong for a guest, listen to their feelings first, then deal with the situation.
5. Follow these seven steps (in order) to make things right: listen, review with the guest what you think they said, empathize,

apologize, resolve, follow up with the guest, and discuss the situation with the team so you can learn from it.

6. If the guest becomes irrational because of the situation, there's a good chance there will be no clean resolution. All you can do is humble yourself, listen, and avoid becoming defensive.

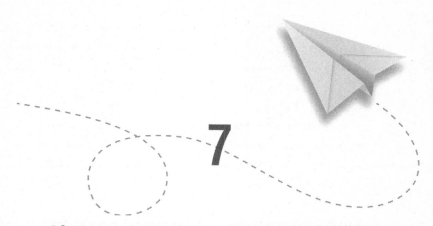

Observe Details, Because Everything Communicates

I'm sure you remember the fictional character Sherlock Holmes. He was an English detective created by Sir Arthur Conan Doyle. He had a knack for walking into a crime scene and seeing things nobody else saw. Even the most seemingly insignificant details told him a clear narrative of what happened at a crime scene.

Although none of us are probably quite as astute as Mr. Holmes, we all adopt his methodologies at times—even if only on a subconscious level. For instance, think of the last time you walked into a room where it was obvious an argument had just occurred. Both of the arguers probably stopped talking as soon as they heard you open the door. But some subtle clues in the room indicate what just happened. You could see micro facial expressions. You could see flushed faces. There was a certain cold courtesy in the way the two interacted with each other. They were trying to pretend like nothing happened, but every single one of those details communicated to you a different story. Even if only subconsciously, most everyone can pick up on those small signals and piece together a story explaining what might have happened.

Just like everything communicates in a crime scene or in a room in which an argument just occurred, everything communicates to your guest. Every small detail they encounter when they engage with your ministry tells them a story—even if it's a story contrary to what you're hoping to tell.

What does the flow of the service communicate to the guest? What does your team communicate? What does your building or room decor communicate?

▶ JONATHAN

One of my biggest pet peeves working at my church had to do with things that were lying around the worship center. For instance, our ushers were in the habit of putting the offering baskets under the seats on the back row of the room. For them, this was the most convenient way to be ready at a moment's notice to receive the offering. But every time I entered the room—especially during a service—I disliked seeing those there. To me, it communicated to a guest that we *really* wanted their money. Or worse, it communicated that we were too lazy to put the baskets in their proper place. The floor is rarely the proper place for anything.

I also disliked things on the stage that weren't in use. A simple example was a microphone stand nobody was using. A bigger example was a grand piano off to the side of the stage that wasn't even touched throughout the whole service. To me, any time I saw something onstage or out in the open, I assumed it would be used at some point during the church service. If nobody used it, it distracted me. It made the whole room feel like a multipurpose room. It cheapened the experience for me.

Most of my fellow staff members thought I was too nitpicky. But if everything communicates, I wanted to make sure everything communicated the story I wanted our church to tell.

■ ■ ■

In *The Starbucks Experience*, Joseph Michelli says, "If you ignore the smaller things that are important to those you serve, you'll fail to create the experience they crave."[1] People crave care and they crave excellence. Is the flow of your ministry communicating that?

► JASON

The same Ritz-Carlton that accommodated my checkout needs thoroughly impressed me with their attention to other small details. Down in the pool area, there was a restroom that connected between the pool and the exercise area. Normally, you wouldn't expect much from a restroom in that type of area. In fact, you might assume it would be pretty disgusting—between all the sweat and chlorinated water that probably dripped all over the facilities. But I noticed this restroom was in impeccable condition.

Even the quality of the paper towels I used to dry my hands impressed me. They were a thicker, expensive quality. In this area where they could have gotten away with something cheaper, they didn't. And that communicated so much to me. Something as simple as paper towels in a bathroom communicated excellence.

■ ■ ■

Often, churches are known for cutting corners. I mean, the church *is* a nonprofit organization after all. Right? But when we choose the easy way out, it communicates a lower level of care to our guests. It communicates that "just okay" is acceptable. Who wants to go to a *just okay* church service? Or a *just okay* youth group? A *just okay* small group? A *just okay* membership class?

Everything communicates to the guest. *Everything.* Here are a few things that might be talking to your guest:

- **The volume of the ambient music in the room.** If it's too loud, it communicates the place is a raucous party. If it's too soft, it communicates the place is a funeral.
- **The colors you paint the walls.** Colors evoke certain emotions in people's minds. What emotions do your walls evoke? Serenity? Anger? Passivity? Excitement?
- **Tissues sitting in front of the stage.** Are you expecting lots of crying during the service? What's going to trigger all these tears? Or is it simply allergy season?
- **The door to a Sunday school or children's church room.** Are there windows in the door or around the room? If not, it might be intimidating for a first-time guest to walk into a room. Or worse, if it's a children's church room, it might be scary for a parent to leave their child in a room with a worker when it appears there's no accountability of people being able to see into the room.
- **The smells in the room.** Those special mini quiches might taste great, but if the kitchen is close to where people will gather, it might stink up the whole room. Or if, before your home group, you cooked a delicious curry meal, there's a good chance that strong smell is still lingering when your guests arrive.

The Importance of Intentionality

Understanding that everything communicates means you need to plan ahead. It's easy to simply make decisions in the moment because decisions *have to* be made. But when you don't make decisions with intentionality, you can't easily control what those decisions will communicate.

The problem is most people don't notice intentionality. It's easy to think some things just happen. Take, for instance, the FedEx logo. By now, you've probably discovered for yourself the hidden arrow between the last "e" and the "x" of the logo. (If not, Google the FedEx logo on your phone. We'll wait.) The white space between the two letters creates an arrow pointing to the right. Do you think that was simply a happy accident? Most people probably imagine the designers opening Photoshop, writing out the word "FedEx," and noticing the arrow it created. "Sweet! Let's make this word two different colors then ship it off to the marketing director!" Most of us think the designers created the whole logo in less than an hour.

It's easy to imagine that happening because that's often how things happen at churches. Faced with weekly, staggering deadlines, we often rely on happy accidents rather than painstaking intentionality. In some ways, it's the nature of the beast of church work.

The truth is, though, the company that worked on the FedEx logo consisted of two or three teams that developed around two hundred concepts for the logo. Some included arrows in the designs, but a simple arrow in a logo didn't communicate what they wanted. The designer, instead, combined two fonts to get the hidden arrow that communicated the story he wanted to tell through the logo. Then he tweaked and re-spaced and re-formed the letters until he got the shape he desired. When he sent it to the bigwigs at FedEx,

119

corporate wanted to make the arrow a bigger deal. They wanted to use the arrow on print pieces and focus on the arrow. But the designer never wanted it to be about the arrow. The arrow was merely a detail that communicated—one of many. And through this high attention to detail, it's still one of the most celebrated logos in history.[2]

What's most interesting about the FedEx logo is that the arrow technically isn't there. It's visible only in the white space. Sometimes, what you *don't* do communicates just as much as what you *do*. What isn't in the picture is just as important as what is. Intentionality takes into account every single element of the experience.

It's easy for people to plan ahead when it comes to big-picture things only. They know generally what will happen at a church service or an event. And that's good. We've all been to churches that obviously haven't even planned the big-picture stuff. But very few churches plan out the details until the last minute. This leads to situations like this:

Team: We need to order communion wafers for this weekend.

Usher: Cool, I'll order something on Amazon.

Looks through Amazon's communion wafer selection.

Usher: These will work. They're the cheapest.

Ordered. The communion wafers arrive and they taste like cardboard.

When you aren't intentional and you don't plan ahead, you'll often choose the cheapest option instead of the best option. Now, that isn't to say that the most expensive option is always the right option. In fact, planning ahead often allows you to stay within budgetary constraints while still integrating excellence into your church service.

120

Often, last-minute decisions are the most expensive decisions. And the options available in the last minute are rarely good choices.

The same is true for businesses. A little bit of planning on the front end will take your guest experience to the next level and save you from future headaches. Think through what the little details will communicate to your customer.

The benefits of forethought allow you to ensure you're happy with what you communicate to your guests. And the best way to do that is to storyboard your guest's experience at your ministry. Walk through their approach scene by scene (refer to chapter 5), and even walk through what the guest will experience through the event or church service. Start with the big picture, then begin integrating details into the whole experience. Walking in the shoes of the guest helps you determine what you need to communicate in each portion of the experience.

The Inconvenience of Intentionality

The problem with intentionality is that it's inconvenient for you. That's something you do want to communicate to the guest, though. You want to communicate that you're willing to be inconvenienced in order to make a great experience for them.

▶ JONATHAN

I always cringe whenever I see a church guest card that has a section labeled "For Office Use Only." For many churches, the guest card is one of their first points of contact with a guest. They're asking a first-time guest to trust them with their private information. But this simple "For Office Use Only" section tells them that this form is designed more for the administrative department than it is for the guest.

121

It tells the guest that they want to make it easy to process their information—unintentionally telling the guest they are simply part of a process, not treated like a human being. Nobody wants to be processed. "For Office Use Only" is the type of thing you see on an IRS form. It isn't the type of thing you want on a card meant to welcome a first-time guest to your church.

■ ■ ■

Removing that "For Office Use Only" section from the guest card introduces inconvenience for the administrative office. There's no consistent place to mark that the guest card was processed and sent to the appropriate destination. It's a slight inconvenience. But a simple stamp on the back of the card or a sticky note could remedy that situation. It's more work, but it's worth it in order to communicate the correct thing to the first-time guest.

Any time you approach anything in your ministry—especially something for guests—from the mentality of "it's better for us internally," you're communicating something negative to the guest. If you're creating a hurdle for the guest because it's convenient for you, you won't like the results of what that says about you.

▶ JASON

Recently I took my family to an amusement park. We were deep into the park when my wife turned to me and asked, "Did you get a map to show us where everything is?"

I hadn't. So I approached a park employee and asked if they had any available for us. "No sir, we don't have those here. Those are at the front of the park."

That created an immediate frustration. *You don't have those? What if someone forgets one like I did? What if their map gets wet? This amusement park is meant for families, yet you didn't anticipate the type of thing that commonly happens in a family situation?*

So I made the lengthy trek back to the front of the park. The only maps available were in an area behind massive lines. In fact, I had to walk out of the main entrance to even find a map. I had to stand in the registration line even though I had already gotten into the park. The fact that they didn't provide maps around the park indicated to me that they were more concerned with not wasting paper than with providing a great experience for my family and me.

Would it have been wasteful to stock maps all around the park? Maybe. But that's an inconvenience that's worth the trouble for what it communicates to the guest.

■ ■ ■

When an organization is unwilling to inconvenience itself for the guest, there's a massive breakdown in the guest's experience. But on the flip side, when an organization goes out of its way to do something for the guest, that creates a memorable moment.

► JASON

For instance, I had a subscription to Birchbox for several years. It's a service that sends toiletries and beauty products to its subscribers each month for a small fee. One month, they left an item out of an order. I emailed them to let them know and asked that they send me the product.

Within an hour I received a response: "I'm so sorry. I sent it out today."

I was impressed with their quick recovery time. But they went on: "I'm also going to add 50 points to your account that you can use toward a purchase."

I never asked for this. I wouldn't have missed it if they hadn't offered it, because I simply wanted the product I was missing. But that extra effort communicated that they understood my inconvenience. They chose to inconvenience themselves in order to make up for the extra trouble they caused me—little as it was.

■ ■ ■

Being intentional puts the extra effort on you. It inconveniences you to make a more memorable experience for the guest. And isn't that the way it should be? When you invite someone over to your house, you don't ask them to cook or to serve the food. You don't give them the uncomfortable chair while you sit on the luxurious couch. You go out of your way to care for them, and that communicates that they're valued. That communicates that their comfort is more important than your own.

Communicating to the Senses

One of the things that made Sherlock Holmes such a brilliant detective was the way he relied upon all five senses to solve the case. He listened to the sounds. He smelled the scents. He touched the evidence. He observed the nuances.

Human beings process through their five senses. So when we talk about everything communicating, we must talk about *how* everything communicates. Your guests will "hear" you through their five senses. That means you'll communicate to them through what they see, hear, smell, touch, and taste.

Historically, churches have focused almost exclusively on sight and sound for communicating to their audience. We concern ourselves with the music and the message—the written word or ornate buildings—to communicate. But over the years, we've neglected the other three senses.

We do a disservice to our message when we do that, though, because people remember things that are designed to tap into all of the senses. Imagine building an experience that includes and considers everything sensory.

Abercrombie & Fitch stores capitalize on this beautifully. They've built an entire shopping experience based on the senses. You show up at the front of the store and are greeted by either a large, half-clothed model on a wall or a real-life, half-clothed model standing there. They pump their signature fragrance through the air conditioning system and their music is blasting loudly enough that you're already in the store before you've even breached the doors. The lighting, the music, the décor . . . they're all communicating something to your senses before you're even aware of the clothes. In fact, the clothes are almost an afterthought to the experience. They realize they're selling an ideal more than an actual product.

While we aren't trying to manipulate impressionable teenagers, guest services teams can learn a lot from that type of five-senses strategy. Consider what you might be communicating to your guests' senses:

Sight

The paint. The flooring. The carpets. The windows. The cleanliness. They all communicate something to your guests. When your guests enter your place of ministry, do they feel the same stress they feel at their own home—feeling the same burden to clean up or fix broken things in their own house? That's probably not a good thing. Or do they feel like they're in a comfortable place that makes sense to them—where they don't feel any extra pressure

125

or responsibility other than to receive? Everything's taken care of for them.

Sound

Does the volume of the music in the lobby or auditorium match the level of the room? If it's too quiet and people are talking loudly, it doesn't match with the energy of the room. If it's too loud and everyone's silent, that's awkward because nobody can connect relationally. The type of music and the volume all communicate something to people before the service even starts.

Unfortunately, we can't give you a specific soundtrack or decibel level for your pre-service music. Those both depend on the type of audience you're reaching and the context of your church. If you're reaching young people, music can be a bit louder with some edgy rhythms. But for older people, you might consider music that's a bit softer. Yet, if the room has cool lighting and haze pumped throughout, quiet Baroque-period music might seem a bit out of place.

Smell

► JASON

One year, during our Easter services, we were planning to show a video that involved a type of tree. The normal fragrance in our church services is nice, but it wouldn't support the visuals they were seeing. So instead, we pumped the scent of a tree through our HVAC system for every service. We wanted to make that video something that was memorable for our guests.

■ ■ ■

That's an over-the-top way of communicating something excellent to your guests. But more simply, think about things like these:

- How do your restrooms smell? Do they smell like public restrooms at a sports stadium?
- What does your room smell like? Fresh paint? Stale air? Does it smell pleasant?
- As a greeter, do you have fresh breath?

The smells in your church are communicating.

Touch

What do your guests feel against their skin when they encounter your ministry? Are the fabrics of the chairs cheap? Does the handout feel like simple copy paper—printed in black and white? Each of those things is communicating something to your guest.

What about physical touch? During some church greeting times, pastors encourage their congregation to hug each other. For some people in some contexts, that might be uncomfortable. For some, even a handshake at the front door might be a bit intimidating. Yet, at a home group, a handshake or hug makes much more sense since it's a personal environment. Be aware of the moment and aware of the context to decide what level of physical touch is appropriate or welcomed.

Taste

What kind of donuts or refreshments do you serve to your guests or volunteers? Are they of cheap quality? Are they generic tasting? What if, instead of those cheap half-and-half containers you buy from Sam's Club, you invested in a carafe with some fresh milk or cold half-and-half? Imagine what that type of quality could communicate to your guests. Or what if instead of just directing

127

people to the water fountain, you offered nice cups and a water dispenser with orange and lemon wedges in it?

As you're planning the details of your ministry, think through ways you can communicate something more memorable through your guests' five senses. When we pay attention to these small details, we ultimately communicate to our guests that we value them. We communicate that we will take good care of them. And that allows them to listen to the next communications—from the emcee, group leader, worship team, pastor, and ultimately, the Holy Spirit speaking individually to each person.

KEY POINTS and TAKEAWAYS

1. Small details in your ministry communicate big things to your guests.

2. Being intentional with small details requires planning those small details ahead of time. The side benefit of planning ahead is that you often get a higher level of excellence for your ministry without paying a premium price.

3. Don't force other people into your way of doing things. Approach your systems from your guest's perspective, even if it means more inconvenience for you and your team.

4. Examine your guest experience from the perspective of all five senses: sight, sound, smell, touch, and even taste. Are the things that influence your guest's senses communicating excellence or a "taking shortcuts" mentality?

8

Reject "Just Okay"

In 1988, Disney released a movie called *Who Framed Roger Rabbit?* It was a revolutionary mixture of live-action and animated characters—created in an era when modern special-effects technologies didn't exist. There's one scene from that movie that's famous in Disney's culture. It's a scene where the main character carries Roger Rabbit into a dark room, and in the process, they bump a hanging lamp.

Of course, the live-action footage shows shadows dancing around the room. But this created a challenge for animators. Would they match those dancing shadows on their drawn rabbit? This would involve incredibly painstaking work. And at that time, when computer-generated special effects were still in their infancy, the audience probably wouldn't have even noticed Roger Rabbit's shadow. The standards for this type of special effect weren't high.

The animators, though, decided it was worth their time to invest into the realism of the movie.

True, it was only one small part of a 103-minute movie. True, they could have gotten away with not adding the shadows and 99 percent of people wouldn't have noticed. But *they* would have known. And they were committed to making the movie excellent from beginning to end, even though this meant hours of extra work. This scene birthed a phrase in Disney's culture: *bumping the lamp*. They refer to bumping the lamp any time they want to go the extra mile to make something excellent. Bumping the lamp means rejecting "just okay" and going above and beyond—even when it's possible nobody will notice the extra effort put into making it excellent.

Imagine if churches put this type of effort into creating excellence for their guests. If a small group leader put this much effort into the meeting. If a youth group did this for high schoolers. It would mean pursuing what is excellent even when it results in extra work that most people might not notice. That's what rejecting "just okay" is about. It's about excellence. And excellence is doing the best you can, all the time. That means creating excellence for the guest during the first impression, the final impression, and every interaction in between.

The problem is, it's tempting to settle for "just okay." Businesses fall victim to this all the time. Over the years, our expectations for customer service have dropped. In fact, even when we get mediocre customer service, we often celebrate it by writing on a comment card. We've become so accustomed to bad service, "just okay" is often an improvement over the norm.

▶ JONATHAN

Here's an example of a time I found myself celebrating "just okay" in a business situation. I recently got the privilege of flying first class on a four-hour flight. I wouldn't have paid the extra $800 for the seat, but I didn't mind taking it when they offered it to me for free.

As I boarded the plane before everyone else, I couldn't help but feel a bit smug as the other passengers watched. Yep, I was about to live the good life for the next four hours. I sat down in my comfortable leather seat (almost as comfortable as a La-Z-Boy), grabbed the headphones to enjoy an in-flight movie, and savored the beverage I was offered before the plane took off.

I pulled out my phone to snap a selfie, and as I was captioning my photo, the ludicrousness of the whole situation struck me. I thought this was the pinnacle of luxury—sitting in a reasonably comfortable seat with decent legroom and getting to enjoy a drink *before* taking off instead of in the air.

I realized I had become so accustomed to the low bar the airlines have set for customer service that I celebrated this as good service. In former years, this was what people expected from an airline—whether in first class or coach. Mind you, that didn't keep me from enjoying the extra relaxation I got during that flight. But it reminded me of how easy it is to begin accepting "just okay."

■ ■ ■

Are you calling something first-class service that should be the bare minimum in your ministry?

Fortunately, this acceptance of mediocrity is starting to change. There are companies starting to understand the "reject just okay" mentality. Consequently, they're starting to magnify the weaknesses of brands that don't provide that level of service. People are starting to notice areas where they became the frog in the boiling pot; they slowly began accepting mediocre customer service from businesses they worked with.

This shouldn't be the reason your ministry chooses to reject "just okay." We aren't trying to be better than for-profit businesses. We want to be better because it affects the guest. It's tempting to believe people don't expect that level of excellence from a church—so we think leaving things at "just okay" is acceptable sometimes.

But the truth of the matter is that the people who visit your church are getting their first glimpse of, yes, your church's brand. Even more than that, though, it's their first glimpse of Jesus. Or maybe they met Jesus at another church, but it was a bad experience. You're ultimately representing the reputation of Jesus Christ to those in your community. Will Jesus be mediocre in his love for his people, or will he be excellent?

Certainly "just okay" doesn't cut it if we are Christ's representatives. That's why it's so important to embrace excellence all the time. It's far more important than customer service; it's how we love others. Excellently.

Where We're Tempted to Settle for "Just Okay"

There are five main areas in which it's tempting to settle for "just okay"—tempting for both you and your team. Let's explore these five areas and see if you or your team has been in any of these situations.

1. When We Think People Won't See

It's tempting to do the bare minimum when you think nobody will see what you're doing. For example, a greeter is standing at his post when he sees the lobby is almost completely empty. There are no guests in sight, so he pulls out his phone to check his text messages or social media accounts. At that moment, a guest walks around the corner. Now the guest has to wait on the greeter. Or worse, they walk right past the greeter and aren't even helped.

The greeter assumed nobody would see, and he might never know that he missed an opportunity with a guest. That experience probably didn't ruin the guest's morning, but it certainly wasn't an excellent experience. If, instead, the greeter had chosen to reject "just okay" in that moment when it appeared nobody would see him, the experience would have been excellent.

2. When Something Just Has to Get Done

▶ JASON

At many of our North Point Ministries campuses, we put mints or a favorite candy in our bathrooms. It's just a small thing we like to provide, knowing it makes the guest feel more confident about interacting with people in the church. You can imagine that those mints or candies disappear quickly, based on the pace and volume of people who come through our services on a given weekend. So one of the responsibilities of our guest services team is to make sure the mint/candy trays are filled all the time. It's a simple, even boring, task. But it's important to the team.

We also have a tray of mints in one of our lobbies, but that one is almost always full because it's visible. The ones in the bathrooms are less visible to the team, so it becomes an out-of-sight/out-of-mind situation. That's one area where we always experience the "just okay" principle. But it's not okay to me.

In fact, my fellow staff members have figured out how much it annoys me. If they see an empty mint basket in the bathroom, they take a picture and send it to me. They know it drives me crazy. It's become such a big joke among the team that I even get pictures when a staff member is out at a restaurant and notices an empty mint basket. They caption it, "Can you come fill this?"

It might only be a mint basket. It's just a task that needs to get done. But when our candy trays are full, it communicates to the guest that we're ready for them.

■ ■ ■

3. When You Don't Feel the Burden for It

If you've ever been around someone in the military, you've probably heard the saying "Close enough for government work." That's the sort of sentiment you hear when something simply *has to* be done and the person doing it doesn't feel the burden for it.

Whenever you stop feeling ownership for your role in welcoming guests, it's easy to accept "just okay." Sometimes a volunteer has never felt the burden for making a guest feel welcome. (Is it up to a worship team to welcome? A youth leader? Janitorial staff? The guy who stocks the coffee bar? Yes. It is.) Others used to have a burden, but it's faded. That's why it's important for leadership to consistently instill the vision of welcoming guests into the team.

When you don't feel the burden, you don't feel the responsibility of it. Then it becomes easy to assume that someone else will do what needs to be done, or that if it doesn't get done it isn't important enough anyway.

4. When It Feels Like the Stakes Are Lower

► JASON

Some of our campuses have some type of early afternoon service. As you might expect, the attendance is lower at those times. Because of the more relaxed environment, the guest services team can potentially mirror that vibe. But I've discovered that when the pace and the volume are lower, it exposes our gaps in service even more.

One weekend, I received a text message from an audio engineer saying he didn't see any ushers at a certain door. I looked for the ushers and saw them sitting down. I asked them to stand up, but I got pushback: "I'll stand up when the guest comes in. It's not that big of a deal."

134

But it *is* a big deal. It says to the guest that you aren't ready for them. And when they come to the door and see you sitting down, it makes them feel like they're interrupting *your* comfort. It's just one guest during a slower service. The stakes feel lower. But the stakes haven't actually changed; only your perception of them has.

■ ■ ■

A guest should never get shortchanged because the stakes seem lower.

- When it's a summer-month service and attendance is low, resist the urge to let things slide here and there. What you do when you think no one's looking matters. (Someone's always looking.)
- If only one or two families show up to the membership class, deliver your very best. If anything, this moment matters even more to the guest since they can easily feel singled out.
- Even though there are no parents checking the sanitization of the toys—and even though that toy never gets the kids' attention—clean it and make it look like the best toy on the shelf. It matters.

5. When You Get Lazy

When you're lazy, either you've become too comfortable with the processes and you settle, or you've decided to cheat/cut corners one time. The problem is, you'll probably get away with it. But when one person cuts corners, others see it. Will they get away with it? Probably. Then another person chooses to cut a corner one time. And gets away with it. Then another.

Soon, one small action snowballs and spreads throughout the whole organization. Allowing "just okay" one time quickly becomes a license to allow it all the time.

We all feel lazy at times. That's normal. But the come back effect requires excellence even when we aren't feeling like it.

Always Improving

If you want to create a culture filled with people who "bump the lamp," you have to create an environment where you're always improving. The standard for excellence tomorrow should not be the same level that it was yesterday. It should be raised incrementally each day.

In fact, that should be the number one reason you *don't* accept when people say, "We've always done it this way." If you've done something the same way for fifty years, that's an indication that you haven't improved in fifty years. Improvement requires processes to change.

Change doesn't have to be drastic, but it should be frequent. Each week should be slightly different than the week before. Sometimes you'll feel like you're taking a step back because you tried something new. That's okay. The true measure of excellence won't be found in one week. True excellence is a long-term move toward better processes and people, even if there are occasional deviations from that trend.

The process of always improving also involves letting multiple voices speak into a situation. Feedback is crucial because it's easy to stop seeing areas where improvement is possible. If you hope to institute a culture of constant improvement, it will require listening to these four voices that can help you improve your processes:

136

1. **Leadership.** If you're the leader, you naturally have the most at stake in creating a culture of constant improvement. You need to listen to yourself when it comes to new ideas on how to improve.

   If you aren't the leader, realize God has given this authority to the leader. Your desire to improve should come from a place of humility and service.

2. **Team members.** Team members are the front line. They hear stories and deal with the frustrations of the processes. A leader should ask their team at least annually for areas where they see potential for improvement.

   Or if you feel the burden for the team and want to be a great help to your leader, encourage your team members to talk to leadership when they see an area for improvement. Approach it with humility. Don't gang up on your leader and criticize. But do communicate areas where you feel things could be better. (Criticism is complaining; critique is offering a solution.)

3. **Guests.** Listen to guests. Don't rely on anecdotal evidence or singular stories, but look for consistently mentioned items. Guests will tell you areas where you can improve through the things they avoid and through subtle things they say.

   If you need to learn more from a guest, be sure you aren't defensive. Then listen and ask insightful questions to see what needs to change.

4. **Other high-level staff members.** (Even if they aren't part of your team.)

When we give permission for all four of those groups of people to speak into the process, we give people permission to create something more excellent. If you're the leader, the first voice is easy to listen to. But the last three can be a bit tougher. It will require humility on your part to listen to those other three—especially other staff members. It requires pretty intense humility to be able to listen to your co-workers or those who work under you.

► JASON

At North Point Ministries, Andy Stanley sends each staff member a survey ninety days and then one year after their hire date. His goal is to get insight from fresh eyes to make the organization better. Andy reads every word of those surveys.

When I got my one-year survey, I worked on it for weeks. I asked several friends and co-workers if my responses made sense. Andy appreciated my survey so much that he called me in for a meeting. He wanted to go over the responses from me and see other ways we could improve.

That shows incredible humility on Andy's part. And that's part of the reason North Point Ministries is still one of the most influential ministries and a beacon of excellence in the church world.

■ ■ ■

Creating an atmosphere of ever-improving excellence requires that sort of humility and a "no sacred cows" approach to evaluation. Everything should be on the table for feedback. And feelings shouldn't get hurt when the feedback happens.

It requires an attitude of wanting to make the situation better, instead of wanting to feel like you did a great job. The sad truth is, constructive feedback will often make you feel like a failure. When you enter into this process of finding places where you can improve, you'll feel like you're doing nothing right.

But you must remember that a few areas of improvement don't undermine the many areas where you do your job well. A squeaky wheel here and there will make the car seem like it's falling apart. But it only indicates a few areas where grease is needed. It's not the end of the vehicle.

Feedback is not an affront to your excellence. In fact, embracing feedback will set a new bar for excellence.

Side note to businesses: When you get feedback from guests, embrace the feedback. They want you to succeed. They actually want to come back to your restaurant or shop or hotel. They're just waiting for you to give them a reason to come back. That reason will be in their feedback.

What Is Excellence?

If we must reject "just okay," what do we embrace instead? What is this excellence we should be working toward? Excellence in the come back effect is:

- **Humble.** If you're full of pride, you won't be willing to listen to input. If you don't listen to input, you won't get the results of excellence.
- **Never ending.** In any journey, there's always an end goal. Unfortunately, in the pursuit of excellence, you'll never fully arrive. There's always a new pinnacle of greatness you can reach.
- **Relentlessly focused on continuous improvement.** If you lose your focus on improvement, you will always settle into a rhythm of autopilot. You'll become comfortable with processes and you'll get "sacred cows." Sacred cows are most often emotional—not actually sacred. They're things like:
  - processes that were set up by a personal hero
  - approaches you saw at that first church where you became a Christ follower, so they feel sacred to you

139

      – obtrusive décor or fixtures that were donated by a founding
      member of the church

      Sacred cows become untouchable assumptions that get
in the way of forward progress.

- **Always thinking about culture.** If you aren't focused on main-taining a culture of excellence, you will always see a drift away from excellence. Excellence is not the default. It has to be fought for. You must constantly ask yourself, "How can we enhance the team's culture? How can we make sure excellence stays part of our culture?"

- **Focused on both the guest *and* the volunteer.** Are you creating an excellent experience for both parties? Or are you focusing on the guest so much that you neglect the volunteers who attend to the guest? A volunteer will generally treat the guest with the same care shown to them.

There was a church who served donuts and coffee to their guests each Sunday morning. They were high-quality, expensive donuts and coffee. The problem was, the volunteers who showed up early always ate all the donuts and drank all the coffee before the guests even arrived.

Unfortunately, instead of simply buying more, they instituted a policy that the volunteers weren't supposed to eat the donuts or drink the coffee at the guest services table. Instead, there were different donuts and coffee available for them in the volunteer room. Of course, those donuts and coffee were not up to the same quality as the ones reserved for the guests.

The volunteers didn't suddenly lash out or become instantly rude. They weren't divas. But that simple gesture communicated a priority to them. It communicated that they were merely tools serving the guests. They didn't have as much value to the church as guests did.

It almost became a sort of competition, where the volunteers eagerly ate the donuts and drank the coffee on Sundays when they weren't serving.

That policy showed lesser care to the people who were supposed to be delivering the care. And it inevitably began to affect the way the volunteers interacted with the guests. Where it was "just okay" to serve subpar treats to the volunteers, it became "just okay" to provide subpar care for the guests.

"Just okay" seems harmless, but it is a virus that will infect your whole ministry if you leave it unchecked. In order for excellence to become the standard, it has to be valued in every single corner and crevice of the organization.

There are five areas where you have the opportunity to create excellence for your guests or simply accept "just okay":

1. **The leader.** Even leaders can be guilty of settling for "just okay." If it's just a season of burnout, it might be time to take a break so you can regain your passion once again. If you've lost the burden, maybe it's time to remind yourself why you got into ministry in the first place—you care about the individual.

2. **The volunteer.** Perhaps the volunteer needs a reminder of the impact they have. Because of who they are—the way they look, act, dress, smile, talk—their welcoming expression can reach someone no other volunteer can reach. And that helps the guest open their heart to experience God through the church service or meeting.

3. **The processes.** The training might be lacking or the tools for recovery might be missing. Maybe it's time to schedule a training session or bring in an outside perspective to refresh the processes.

4. **The culture (internal).** A guest will feel what the volunteer feels. If a volunteer feels that the culture is one of settling, the guest will feel that too. Reach out to volunteers or team members and get their honest perspective on the culture of the ministry. Working on the inside (your culture) influences the impact on others.

5. **The brand (external).** When a guest interacts with team members, they are interacting with the brand of the ministry. If they perceive the volunteer as excellent, they will tend to perceive the brand as excellent. If the volunteer perceives the brand as excellent, they will tend to provide extra excellence. It's a self-fulfilling prophecy. Give the volunteer a reputation to be proud of, and you'll find they live up to that reputation. Do people perceive your church as excellent? Do they perceive your Sunday school class as excellent? Your youth ministry? The kids' program? The small group? The membership class? Or is your ministry's brand one of mediocrity?

As you seek to reject "just okay" in your ministry and reach for excellence, ask yourself the following three questions. Apply them to those five areas. Then continue to ask these questions as you continue to improve your people and your processes.

1. **What's worth starting?** Should you implement a new process or find new tools to help you achieve excellence in the come back effect?

2. **What's worth fixing?** Is there a process that isn't functioning properly that merely needs a tweak or a reorganization to make it work the way it was meant to?

3. **What's worth ending?** If there is something distracting from excellence, it's important to stop it. Is there a policy that gets in the way of your volunteers providing excellent care? Is there something unnecessary that's done in a mediocre way that would be best if your team didn't do?

Excellence is not easy. It's inconvenient. But it's worth the effort to demonstrate the love of God to those he has entrusted to our care.

KEY POINTS and TAKEAWAYS

1. Excellence is doing the best you can, all the time, even when you think no one will notice.
2. Many of the people visiting your church are getting their first glimpse of Jesus. Will that first glimpse be of excellence or of mediocrity?
3. The standard of excellence tomorrow should not be the same level it was yesterday. If you're doing some things because you've always done them that way, it means you haven't been improving in those areas.
4. An atmosphere of continuing excellence requires a "no sacred cows" approach where everything in your ministry is up for discussion and improvement.
5. Three questions will help you find areas where you can improve: What's worth starting? What's worth fixing? What's worth ending? There are some things—even good things—that you should stop doing if they aren't pushing your ministry toward excellence.

9

Choose Values over Policies

► JASON

Daniel serves in the parking area at one of our church campuses. We intentionally put him in the parking lot where parents with preschoolers prefer to park. If you knew Daniel, you'd know why.

Each weekend you'll find Daniel wearing a lime-green vest and waving two light sabers (aka orange light wands) while safely parking cars and helping people walk into the building. The thing that sets Daniel apart, though, isn't necessarily his excellence at performing the task—and he *is* excellent. What sets Daniel apart is his fun dance moves. He gets into it each weekend and has so much fun dancing that parents can't help but smile as they find their parking space.

Daniel takes potentially aggravated parents—dealing with the stress of parking lots and preschoolers complaining in the minivan—and creates a great experience for them. His decision to let his

145

personality shine creates a positive vacation from stress for everyone. In addition, it sends a small message that he loves what he does.

This is a visible embodiment of one of our guest services values: the value of having fun.

■ ■ ■

Values, principles, priorities—whatever you want to call them— are far more valuable than policies, because they evoke responses from team members that you can't manufacture. For instance, you could try to tell your parking lot attendees to dance. But for many, it would seem mechanical or uncomfortable. In Daniel's situation, the "having fun" value allowed him to highlight his unique per-sonality to create a one-of-a-kind experience. Another volunteer might turn this value into juggling or telling quick jokes to people when appropriate. Still for another, it might just mean smiling because she truly enjoys her role.

Values are those ideas, behaviors, and truths we embrace as being the filter through which we make decisions in our orga-nization. Values tell our team members what matters most. When you establish a set of values for your team, you are declaring the important elements of what you believe so you can do what mat-ters. *This is why we do what we do.*

The power in values-driven ministry is that it makes decisions easy for volunteers and staff members. When a situation or ques-tion arises, the team member doesn't have to scroll through a list of policies in their mind or refer to a manual. They can simply reflect back on your organization's values and see whether or not an ac-tion aligns with them. "We value having fun in this organization, so how should I respond to this situation in a way that reinforces that value yet doesn't make the guest feel uncomfortable?"

The truth is, it's impossible to have policies in place that cover every situation. Unexpected things always happen. Hospitality happens in the way you deal with the unexpected.

Think of it like this: Whenever new technology arises, governments have to determine whether they should create new laws to regulate the use of the technology. Consider cell phones in cars. A few years ago, many cities made laws to keep people from talking on their phones while driving. Recently, many cities are adding texting to the list of banned activities. But what about when new technology arises that potentially distracts a driver? What about using the GPS in their phone? What about new heads-up-display technologies? Virtual reality?

When you are a policy-driven organization, you have to make new rules each time a situation arises. In many cases, churches make rules before anything even happens, just in case. But in a values-driven organization, the values don't change. The applications change.

In the situation of cell phones in cars, you could keep making policies:

- Don't reroute your GPS while the car is in motion.
- No using virtual reality headsets while driving, unless the field of vision is at least 120 degrees.
- No applying makeup while the car is in motion.

The list of laws would become ridiculous, because situations keep changing.

Or you could simply say, "As a nation, we value distraction-free driving. Don't drive distracted." That covers texting, phone calls, reading your mail, applying makeup . . . the gamut. For each

147

person, the value manifests itself in different actions and different ways. But one simple value makes it easy to decide. "Will I be distracted by performing this activity? Then I won't do it." The value covers thousands of different potential situations, and it takes the guesswork out of them.

Obviously, values-driven systems don't necessarily work well for governments. But in an organization where the team is carefully crafting training and culture, values can help steer volunteers without having to create a fifty-page manual filled with policies for every potential situation.

Why should your ministry be run by values instead of policies?

- Values last. They aren't created at the whim of trends.
- Values keep you from having lists of constrictive rules. They provide freedom for individuality.
- Values help make things consistent across the organization.

Here are the questions for your ministry: Do you have a list of values? Does your team know the values? Do they know what to do with them? Values should be basic, but they are remarkable when integrated into the behaviors of the organization.

You can coach new team members from the values. You can let people go from the values. You can know what you do as an organization, and you can know what you *don't* do as an organization.

Many organizations have a list of values, but if those values don't permeate everything you do, they're simply nice statements. For instance, if you're pleased with something someone does that contradicts one of your organization's values, your values aren't real values. Or if someone gets in trouble for doing something that aligns with one of your ministry's values, again, your values aren't real values.

Think of greeters in the worship center. If one of your values is "have fun," you can't chastise them for happily chatting with guests because it was too loud for the prayer moment happening after service. You can skillfully suggest they move to a new location. But if there's an edge in your voice, you just killed the "have fun" value by punishing one of your team members for having fun.

This type of thing creates an unstable culture for your organization. People don't really know what will make the leader or team members happy because whims seem to dictate proper behavior instead of values upon which everyone can agree.

It's important to have a short list of values—three or four—that can bring everyone onto the same page when it comes to welcoming guests. They should be simple enough that people can remember them and actually do something about them.

Identifying the Values

▶ JASON

We give our locations autonomy to create their own guest services values. At Buckhead Church, the guest services team has four values: (1) show care, (2) have fun, (3) remain flexible, and (4) deliver wow.

Our guest services team especially excels at value #3 (remain flexible). Depending on our service times and the season of attendance we are in, the people flow varies. Therefore, we pay attention to where the guest needs us—not necessarily where "my spot" is.

I recall Sandra understanding this need. She started out in one spot, moved to another, and then switched again to a different position all within 150 feet of where she originally started. She did all of this within one hour. Why? She paid attention to where the people were going and identified the optimal place for her to stand to help the guest feel the benefit. She was not focused on always being in the same spot each week. Her approach is, "I'll go where I'm needed and while there, I will be flexible to respond to people flow and needs."

■ ■ ■

Buckhead Church allows those four values to direct everything their guest services team does. But your ministry's values might look a little different. Your value statements need to reflect what matters to your organization, to your leadership, and to the people you're trying to reach.

Different organizations use different methods to arrive at their list of values: online assessments, decks of cards that list different values, exploring what matters to the company, uncovering what matters to the leader . . . There are many different ways to go through it, but one of the easiest ways is simply to work through some questions. For instance, if you're the leader, start by creating a personal list of values for your family or life. You might work through questions like these:

- What makes me come alive?
- What makes me feel bad?
- What makes me happy?
- What makes me mad or sad?
- Where have I failed?
- What was it about the failure that made me still come alive and move forward?
- Where have I seen the greatest amount of movement/results?
- When people compliment me or critique me, what do I hear?
- What books do I read the most?

- What things keep me up at night?
- What things do I not really care about? (Don't include those in your list.)
- What things are natural for me?
- What are things I've learned from family members?

Then you simply combine those things into a list of words or phrases that reflect your personal values. Next, process those personal values with what your organization values.

- What matters to the church already?
- What does the church already do well?
- What do we already do for the guest?
- What things do we intentionally *not* do for the guest?
- What might the guest want and know they want?
- What do they want but not know they want?
- What can we do to make the guest feel comfortable, safe, etc.?
- What are the basic needs of a guest?
- Why does a team member want to be part of a team?
- What must happen in the environment that contributes to a remarkable experience?

Then put those things into words and combine your lists. Although you want the values to primarily reflect your organization, the value list you adopt for your team will probably reflect your personality and goals because you're part of the team. If you're a leader, any team will tend to reflect your personality to a small degree, because that's what leadership does—it leaves its fingerprint on things.

151

Finally, begin pruning, combining, and removing from the list. Some of the values will be similar, so combine them. Some of them will seem like good ideas but aren't actually true values for your team or organization. Finally, some of them will be behaviors, not values. You can save behaviors for later; you don't want to include them in your list of values.

Work through these and begin incorporating them into your team.

Note to multisite churches: There's a chance your various campuses will have slightly different approaches when it comes to welcoming the guest. For instance, an urban campus might welcome its guests a bit differently than a rural campus or a suburban campus. Depending on your church culture, though, you might still want to have a unifying core of values that brings your organization together and makes it one entity.

What about if you're a volunteer or team member and your leader hasn't established a list of values? The good news is, you can still figure out your leader's values and implement them in your personal approach to welcoming guests. You can explore the policies already in place, then ask yourself why the policies exist. (Sometimes, this can be difficult if certain policies have been inherited from previous leaders.) Explore the spirit of the rule; that's where you'll find the real value behind the policy.

Even if a leader hasn't verbalized their values, they still have them. They just haven't thought about them yet. You can, with humility, walk your leader through this process and help them discover their own values. Yes, you can revolutionize your team even if you aren't in a leadership position.

Integrating the Values

► JASON

Imagine you're a parent. You bring your child with you to church. For one reason or another, you decide to let them stay with you in the auditorium during the service. Maybe they're afraid to go to the kids' ministry, or you aren't sure you want to stick around for the whole service. Very quickly, though, you discover your child is not as interested in sitting down and being quiet as you were expecting. So you take your child to the lobby to prevent them from becoming a distraction for the rest of the people in the room. You're already a bit embarrassed as you walk into the lobby and find a place to entertain them (and hopefully still participate in the service). What next?

Our guest services team members are constantly watching the auditorium doors for guests who walk out with a child and sit in our open gathering space. Whenever this happens, they can grab a KidPak (which contains a Disney coloring book, crayons, and stickers) and a snack pack of Goldfish crackers for the child. This is something we set up to fulfill our "deliver wow" value. It's a small and tangible way to deal with a situation we know is probably going to happen frequently. Paying attention by doing the small things really well allows guests to feel cared for even as they feel frustrated because they have to leave the service.

■ ■ ■

It's important to empower the team to act out your ministry's values. A KidPak is the perfect way to give your team tools to deliver a wow.

Whenever you set a list of values for your team, behaviors need to follow. If not, you simply created a nice list of phrases that will

153

live on a wall somewhere until some archeologist digs it up in the distant future.

So how do you go from a list of platitudes to an active, breathing list of values that affects everything your team does? Here are ten steps to help leaders turn their values into a reality.

1. Live them.

If one of your values is to have fun, the leader needs to set the tone for that. It's nearly impossible for a volunteer to have fun when their leadership is stressed out. If you're the leader, create a fun environment for your team. Laugh with them. Don't stress out when someone shows up late. Don't ice people out when they're unavailable when you need them. Model the behavior you're trying to see in your team.

As the team sees their leader living out the values, they'll follow along.

2. Teach them.

Great leaders teach these values to their team and teach them often. One pastor said, "Repetition is the price of knowledge." It often takes at least three times for someone to hear something before they actually understand what they're hearing.

Then teach the values in different ways. Some people are auditory learners, meaning they need to hear it. Some are visual, meaning they need to see it. Still others are kinesthetic, meaning they need to participate in the learning process. Present the values in different ways each time you teach them so you can make sure everyone catches them. You might even consider printing out a gigantic, beautiful poster with the values and plastering it on the walls of the volunteer room.

3. Acknowledge them when you see them in team members.

People place value on the things you praise. So make sure you're praising the correct things.

For instance, if parents raise a young daughter always telling her how beautiful she is, that child will grow up believing beauty is of utmost importance. She'll believe that being beautiful is the way to make people happy with her. Thus her life will center on beauty. However, if those parents instead praised things like integrity, honesty, and bravery, those would become the focus of her life—even into adulthood.

While you might not have the same impact on your team members as a parent raising a young child, your praise will ultimately determine what your team values (even if you aren't the leader). When you praise a team member for embodying one of your team's values, others will see it and naturally adopt that same value in their own conduct.

4. Identify creative and memorable ways to communicate them.

One of the things Jesus did that made his teachings so memorable was telling stories. He even made them shocking at times—making the assumed villain become the hero of the story (such as in the Good Samaritan). There's something about stories and the unexpected that sticks in our minds. Use these story devices to make your values memorable for your team.

If you're the leader, you might even consider empowering your team to brag on their fellow team members in a meeting. "How have you seen a team member demonstrate these values?" Highlight and celebrate those wins that reinforce your values.

5. Invite people onto the team who already live out the values.

If you see someone in your church demonstrating these values, invite them onto your team. (People in your congregation who already work in customer service are great options.) You'll often find this sparks excitement in them, knowing that your team is looking for behaviors like theirs. What a great thing for a church to call out God-given aptitudes in its members!

Plus, if you're starting from scratch with a new set of values, these new team members can become great examples for the team. You can refer to them in moments of teaching or encourage them to challenge their teammates to do what they do.

Often, people will never have even considered volunteering. A simple invitation might be all they need.

6. Create ways for team members to participate in a value.

Empower your team to do things that support the values. For instance, the KidPaks in Buckhead Church's lobbies make it easy for the guest services team to deliver wow. As you train your team and make these types of tools available, you're further reinforcing your belief in the values. Plus, you make the values tangible with a specific way they can be turned into a behavior.

7. Talk with leaders about what happens when values don't go well.

Just like you want to paint a vision of what could happen if the values work in conjunction with behavior, explain what can happen when they don't work. Personalize the stories you tell. Chances are, most of your team members will be able to empathize with a story you tell; we've all been victims of poor customer service or uncomfortable church experiences.

8. Attach behaviors to each value.

This is where you can bring back your list of behaviors you removed when you were making your list of values. Under each value, make a list of supporting behaviors.

► JASON

The guest services values at Buckhead Church have supporting behaviors that look like this:

- Show Care
  - Anticipate and fulfill needs.
  - Acknowledge each person.
  - Intentionally listen and respond appropriately.
  - Give a warm greeting and good-bye.
- Remain Flexible
  - Provide quick service recovery.
  - Find a gap and fill it.
  - Support each other.
  - Use autonomy inside our framework to problem-solve.
- Have Fun
  - Share a smile.
  - Have a joyful attitude.
  - Show elements of your personality.
  - Keep interactions upbeat and positive.
- Deliver Wow
  - Do little things really well.
  - Make personal connections with people.
  - Create surprise-and-delight moments.
  - Think through nonverbal gestures.

■ ■ ■

9. Give and receive feedback through the filter of the values.

Something will go wrong. You can expect that. When something goes wrong, as much as possible, tie the error back to the values. "What happened today wasn't a good example of *showing care*. Here's how we could have done it differently." Behaviors are much easier to correct when you show people the "why" behind the desired behavior. Your values are the why.

10. Give team members incremental steps on aligning with values.

Never criticize a team member who's misaligned with the values. In *How to Win Friends and Influence People*, Dale Carnegie suggests this: "Use encouragement. Make the fault seem easy to correct."[1] When you provide simple, tangible steps of improvement to a team member, it gives them something to aim for. Nobody wants to feel like a situation is hopeless, especially if they're volunteering their time. Give them hope that they can fit into the team, and show them how to do it.

Keep the Values Alive

Once you've integrated these values into your ministry, revisit them often. Don't let them become just another mission statement or vision statement that sits on a plaque or a paper only to collect dust. Filter every single thing your team does through these values and keep them fresh for your organization. That'll mean dropping some behaviors that don't align with your values. That'll also mean tweaking your values to align with some of the behaviors you want to see happen in the team.

▶ JASON

After one of our training sessions, one of my new team leaders approached me. He said, "You really believe all this, don't you? You believe these four things can guide what we do and make us successful."

I do.

My passion for these values translated to that leader. He saw and felt that I really meant what I was saying. And that translated to his team. When we value the values, our team values them too. They'll see it, they'll catch it, and the values will spread.

■ ■ ■

You'll know your team members have internalized the values when they start coming up with their own creative ideas. "I know one of our values is 'have fun,' so I thought it would be a great idea to give our parking lot team colorful signs that say things like 'welcome,' 'looking good today,' and 'so glad you're here.'" When your team members surprise you with new ideas that reinforce the values, you'll know they value the values.

They'll also be quick to point out policies that conflict with the values. If you're a leader, be willing to hear those critiques and make changes when necessary. You can't allow policy to win over values.

KEY POINTS and TAKEAWAYS

1. Policy-driven organizations have to make new rules each time a situation arises. Values-driven organizations, on the other hand, can help steer volunteers without having to create a fifty-page manual filled with policies for every potential situation.

2. Your real values won't necessarily match your written values. Real values are the things you praise and the things you discipline.

3. Values are different from behaviors. But a great statement of supporting behaviors can help cast the vision for your values.

4. There are ten great ways to integrate your values into your organization:

   a. Live them.

   b. Teach them.

   c. Acknowledge them when you see them in team members.

   d. Identify creative and memorable ways to communicate them.

   e. Invite people onto the team who already live out the values.

   f. Create ways for team members to participate in a value.

   g. Talk with leaders about what happens when values don't go well.

   h. Attach behaviors to each value.

   i. Give and receive feedback through the filter of the values.

   j. Give team members incremental steps on aligning with values.

Reach for Significance

You'll notice in this book we never once mentioned the topic of teamwork, even though teamwork is vitally important. Through the collective effort of a team you can achieve something far bigger than what you could accomplish on your own.

You see this in sports every day. Teams that work together win together. Some players get more glory, but each member puts in equal effort—defensively, offensively, and in their hustle. On the other hand, you'll see teams plagued with all-star syndrome that can't seem to get their act together. They rely fully on the team's champion to make all the big plays. Consequently, it all rests on the shoulders of one person.

► **JONATHAN**

In college, I was somewhat of an all-star. My college group met in an old, repurposed McDonald's the church owned. It was a multipurpose building, which meant we had to set everything up each Friday and tear it down after the service. We weren't just creating a casual meeting with a few chairs, a guy on a guitar, and a djembe. It was a full-blown, seeker-sensitive, light show / fog machine, stage-setup-intense service. Hundreds showed up each week. I was the volunteer worship leader, so I felt the biggest burden for making the production as awesome as it could be.

That translated to me showing up at 4:00 p.m., by myself, and spending the next three hours setting everything up. I lugged out the sound system, the lighting rig, the stage boxes . . . everything by myself. Then I wired it all up, rushing to be ready for rehearsal at 7. The service began at 8.

The rest of the teams showed up an hour before service to do their jobs—totally uncommitted to the cause (at least that's how I felt).

I continued like this for three years—pouring hours of work into my job. I'd like to think the ministry made huge strides because of my efforts. But when it was time for me to step out of my position and move on to something else, this area of ministry hadn't progressed one bit. The processes hadn't improved. The quality wasn't any better. It still all rested on one person's shoulders to make it all happen. It was a struggle to find the person who could handle that type of pressure.

You see, I failed to empower anyone else to carry the torch for the ministry. I never trained anyone to take my place or even, at the very minimum, assist me. Consequently, I couldn't take a weekend off without the college service suffering greatly.

Other teams grew. Their jobs even seemed to get easier as more people came on board to carry the load. But I was always there at 4:00 p.m. and grew resentful that nobody else was committed like me. I had all-star syndrome, and that translated to everyone else on my worship team. They knew I'd handle things. It wasn't their fault they didn't show up early; I never gave them the opportunity to. It was easy for them to fade into the background and let me bear the brunt of the responsibility. That's not how teamwork works.

I didn't succeed as a leader, because I failed to make each team member feel significant. I let the service rest on my own shoulders instead of highlighting the importance of each person's role. Even though I had a "team," there was no true team dynamic.

■ ■ ■

The key to a strong team is each member understanding their own significance—both as an individual and in their role. It's one of the main things everyone wants, but unfortunately, many people fail to feel that level of significance as an employee or volunteer. However, when a team feels significant, that becomes the tipping point toward taking the teamwork dynamic to the next level.

All-star syndrome plagues many churches and ministries. It's important to give people responsibilities and let each member contribute what they're best suited to offer. When you've done that, it's a great start. But just because you've brought people on board and spread the load doesn't mean you've perfected the team dynamic.

Often, ministries tend to focus on need instead of significance. They *need* someone to watch the kids. They *need* a Sunday school leader or parking lot attendant. There's a missing piece in the ministry machine and frankly, it doesn't matter who fills it. This can lead a volunteer or team member to feel more like a cog in the wheel than a valued team member. There's no significance in being an easily replaceable machine part.

► JONATHAN

I experienced this volunteering on a production team at a large church. They had eight roles each week they needed filled. I was one of those roles, and I did my job well. But on occasion I had to go out of town for work. Because the team was understaffed—as are almost all volunteer teams at churches—I felt guilty that I couldn't fulfill my role that week. The ministry leader made sure I fully realized that guilt, too, by mentioning how much they needed me and the hole I would leave in the team. Everyone else would have to scramble to make up for what I couldn't accomplish that week.

Consequently, that led me to start feeling a sense of guilt every time I couldn't be part of the team. I realized how important it was to have eight people on the team, and my not showing up added further burden to the team. That feeling began to build each time I couldn't contribute on a weekend. I ultimately began to associate that volunteer position with a sense of guilt. Then that eventually transferred to the church. I felt like I was walking on eggshells whenever I attended.

Volunteering for a church shouldn't create a sense of obligation or guilt. That's discouraging and eventually wears team members out. But that's what happened to me. I eventually left the volunteer team feeling discouraged.

Later, however, I volunteered at a different church. Instead of focusing on the need I filled by volunteering, they focused on the significance of the job. More than that, they focused on my significance in that role. I found when I had to miss a week, I no longer felt guilty. I felt like I was missing out on a good thing. I knew the team was having to scramble a bit without me there, but they didn't make me feel like a bad volunteer. Instead, I missed the feeling of significance I got when I was functioning in my role as part of the team.

When I finally got back to the team the following week, I was even more grateful to be part of the process. I felt rejuvenated and ready to tackle my tasks again. And it was all because of feeling significant over feeling needed. Significance is the key.

■ ■ ■

We're all looking for significance, so much so that we'll even give up good things in order to feel that thrill of importance. You see this all the time in churches—a wealthy businessman or professional quits a high-paying job and joins the church staff making far less money. Because they find significance in their role—a significance they never found in the marketplace—they substitute "success" for the joy and fulfillment of working with a church.

The feeling of significance made them glad to sacrifice pay because significance is an innate human need. At some point, more money doesn't add much value to your life. But more significance does.

In any job someone performs—whether volunteer or paid—they want to feel:

- like their work is important.
- like they are bringing something unique and valuable to the job.
- like they're excellent in their job and are the right person for their role.
- that their leaders and their co-workers value their effort.

Those four things are the keys to feeling significant in any given role. And when a team member feels that, they feel like they're part of a team that's doing something worthwhile. Thus they're happy to function in their given role.

However, when a team member doesn't feel significant in their role, the whole team begins to break down. One bad apple really will spoil the whole bunch. A lack of feeling significant will look like this for a volunteer:

- "Showing up" is enough for them.
- They aren't actively inviting others to join the team.
- They'll see something that needs to be done but leave it for someone else.
- They begin devoting time elsewhere to the neglect of their role—like late-night events that cause them to be tired when they show up for their duty the next day.

Feeling significant is often the thing that turns an unmotivated worker into the most motivated person on the team.

Stop right now and evaluate yourself. Do you feel significant in your role? Or do you feel more like a cog in the ministry machine?

If you're a leader, ask yourself how your team members feel. Are they merely interchangeable machine parts? Or is there a sense of "missing out" when they have to be absent one week? Is significance a part of your ministry?

How Churches See Volunteers, and How Volunteers See Churches

Traditionally, churches have seen volunteers as a tool to serve the guest. Many churches focus on the guest so much that they actually forget about the volunteer. When the volunteer isn't serving, they're a guest again and the church can pour into them. But when they're serving, they merely become a tool of the church.

► JASON

I'm ashamed to say I was that person for a time. I used volunteers to achieve something. I was interested in the volunteer, but I was more interested in the mission that was greater than the volunteer. Many years ago, I was even willing to use a volunteer in order to achieve the mission, because I was a results guy. Since then I've been on a journey to discover what it's like to value the guest *and* the volunteer.

■ ■ ■

If you're a leader, we hope you haven't fallen into this trap—but it's easy to start gravitating toward it. It's easy to see volunteers as a commodity to be used instead of as actual people. And when this happens, significance goes out the window.

It's sad, because volunteers typically see churches as a place where they can feel significant. It starts out that way—volunteering in order to feel like they're a part of something bigger than themselves. And that's often how we market volunteering to our congregations: "Feel significant by being part of a team." They start seeing the church as an organized, perfect team with perfect people, perfect leaders, perfect processes . . . Of course, if you've been involved in churches for very long, you know it's not that way. The church is filled with imperfect, broken people trying their best to love other broken people. But that's not what the volunteer was expecting, so they can quickly become disillusioned. We unintentionally sell volunteers on an experience that's not actually what they get.

Imagine if churches instead saw volunteerism as an opportunity to help their volunteers understand personal significance. Churches would see the volunteer's role as less important than their growth.

"Firing" a volunteer wouldn't be about them not having value; it would be motivated by a desire to see them thrive in a role perfectly suited for their gifts and talents.

It's like a father who asks his son to help him work on a project. Yes, the father actually needs his son's help. And yes, the father is going to expect a level of excellence from the son. But a good father isn't as concerned with the project as he is the growth of his son. He wants to teach his son values like hard work, persistence, and excellence. The project is merely a vehicle to help the son grow into a better person. It's also an opportunity for the father and son to grow closer in their relationship.

Imagine if ministries approached volunteers more like that. How significant do you think we could make a team member feel?

► JASON

I recently experienced this with one of my team members. There was a man who found so much fulfillment and significance in his role in the guest services team that he actually filtered his career choices through his experience here.

The man approached me asking for my advice. There were two job opportunities available to him. One offered more money and more promise, but it would require him to sacrifice his values a bit. The other job was a good job, but it certainly wasn't as glamorous as the first. Because of the significance he felt in his role at the church and because he felt that I saw him as significant, he approached me with the decision. Of course he knew which decision was the right one. But it made me feel honored to know he trusted me so much as a leader that he wanted me to talk to him about this decision he was about to make.

■ ■ ■

168

When we start seeing each volunteer as a gift that God has given us to steward—just like a good father would see his children—we're on the right track to making each volunteer feel significant. And with that significance, our teams will blossom.

Creating a Culture of Significance

The evolution of significance in each team member should look like this:

1. They matter in their role.
2. They matter beyond their role.
3. They matter.

As a volunteer joins the team, they should realize first and foremost they're important in their role. If they don't realize that, they won't feel significant at all. Next, though, they should start feeling like they're significant even apart from their work. They matter to the ministry even if they don't perform their role. Finally, though, the ultimate significance comes from realizing they simply matter—to God, to the ministry, to the leadership.

The ultimate significance happens when you realize you are important and valuable—even if you never did anything significant at all. That's the place a good leader should take them in their identity with God. When a volunteer learns to rest in their unconditional significance to God and to the leader, it takes away the pressure of performance. It's no longer an obligation; it's an opportunity. The way they perform their duties becomes a gesture of love and gratitude.

How do you get there? Here are some ideas on creating a culture of significance in your team—whether you're a leader or just someone trying to influence the culture of your team. (Yes, you can lead even if you aren't the one in charge.)

Ask, "Why Do People Volunteer?"

Obviously, the answer is to feel significant. But what is it about a particular role they volunteered for that will make them feel significant? Is it their ability to connect with people? Is it their desire to make people feel comfortable? Is it their passion for systems and helping things run smoothly?

Often, people volunteer because they experienced something negative in another ministry, and they want to change that experience for other people. Find out what that experience was. Then empower them to create a great experience for others instead of what they felt. "What have you seen done badly, and how can we do things better?"

On the other hand, some volunteers might step up because they experienced something positive. They want to help others experience that same thing. Discover what that good experience was, then empower the volunteer to repeat that experience for other guests. "What have you experienced that you wish you could do for others?"

The responses to this question will likely be simple. But the answers will help you get better at inviting people to join the team.

Ask, "How Can We Focus on Enhancing the Significance of Each Guest?"

People want to help other people. It gives a person fulfillment to know that they were the only one who could have possibly helped—and they did. People stand up straighter when they do this. When a guest feels significant, the volunteer can feel significant.

It's fulfilling. When you put a special focus on the significance of the guest, it becomes part of the culture. *If my leader sees the guest as more than just a number, I wonder what they see in me . . .*

Ask, "What Are the Needs of Every Volunteer?"

As you meet the needs of your volunteers, they'll see that they are significant to you. Some of the needs volunteers have are:

- Communication that is clear, helpful, accurate, and repeatable.
- Encouragement that is specific.
- Resources that help your volunteers be healthy, efficient, and effective.
- Measurable "wins" so that they know when they did things right.
- Team identity that helps a volunteer understand their role in the team.
- Team spirit. (Everybody wants to be proud of their own team.)
- Feedback channels where a volunteer knows they will be heard.

You can provide these things to your team whether you're the leader or a team member. Think through ways you might do this.

Discover the Best Way to Make a Volunteer Feel Loved

If you've read Gary Chapman's *The 5 Love Languages*, you know that different people experience love differently. So saying "You did a great job" might mean more to one volunteer than to another.

Figure out how each volunteer feels most loved and appreciated, and look for appropriate ways to express that love and appreciation to them. (You might want to be careful if their love language is physical touch.)

Look for Ways to Be Personal

Personally care for your team members. Remember details about their lives.

► JASON

I was talking to a dad one day about the paint on the walls, when he mentioned that he was heading north soon to drop his daughter off for college. It had nothing to do with the conversation, but I remembered that detail. The next week, I was able to say, "I know you mentioned taking your daughter to college last week. What was that like? You had her for eighteen years and now she's at college. How are you feeling this week?"

It had nothing to do with his role or his ability to do it well, but I genuinely cared about him. And that personal conversation meant so much and went far toward making him feel significant.

■ ■ ■

Empower Team Members

If you're the leader, give away responsibility and authority. One of the most motivating factors for a worker is the ability to make their own decision and to have their leaders back them up in that decision. If all decisions must run through the leader, the volunteer won't feel significant in their role.

Instead, trust your team members and support them in their decisions. If you must correct a wrong decision, do it after the fact—not in the moment. Wait until after the service or once the guest has left the environment. This allows your team members to save face; it also will help you calm down so your correction doesn't come across as frustration or anger.

Business owners have long known the value of correcting team members quickly and privately, but make sure there's been enough time for the emotions of the situation to settle down. Be sure you fully know what went wrong and how to fix the problem. And, pro tip, ask your team member how they think they could do better next time. They might have valuable insight that you've never considered. This gives them ownership over improvement.

Hold Them Accountable

Check up on what you assign to your team members. As a volunteer, I want to know if I was successful. Don't let your team members guess if they did things well or not.

Give good feedback to your team members about their performance. Then challenge them to do even better at their job. People love to know what you expect from them.

Celebrate Significance over Results

It's easy to celebrate quantifiable results when you talk to your team. "Things ran well. We're adding fifty people to our team." Those are measurable and visible. But those don't work toward making your volunteers feel significant.

Instead, focus on the impact that your volunteers had on people's lives. "Last week, Susie, you talked to someone who had never stepped foot in a church. She told us all about how welcomed you made her feel. Great job. You made a lasting impact on her."

It's great to recognize and reward people. But when you help people discover their significance, that's lasting.

Your Significance

Ultimately, the most important thing you can do to help make your team members feel significant is for *you* to feel significant. As a leader, if you don't feel significant, how could you possibly hope to make your team feel significant? Whether you're in an official leadership position or just lead the team in the example you provide, it's important that you understand you have value beyond your role in the ministry.

It's easy to define our value and significance based on the work we do. If we do a good job as a leader, we have value. Unfortunately, that also means that if something goes wrong or if someone is unhappy with us, we feel that we have no value.

It's unfortunate, because your true significance is not found in your success at your job. After all, what happens when that's taken away from you? What happens when you lose your job? When you're forced to retire? When you get injured and can no longer perform the task? Every role we assume in life is temporary, so we can't find our identity in that.

The apostle Paul was a tentmaker. Peter was a fisherman. Jesus was a carpenter. But their legacy far exceeded their jobs. They were called to bigger things than their roles. They didn't find their identity in those things.

That isn't to say they weren't faithful in their jobs. We have to work hard at everything we do. But we have to realize our significance is bigger than just our job.

▶ JASON

There was a time in my ministry when I didn't feel significant. When I didn't feel it, I couldn't make others feel significant. I've been that guy for a few reasons: a mean pastor or a cutthroat work environment. Others' words had caused me to start questioning myself, and it got difficult to feel significant on the team. That's a very unhealthy place to be. Ultimately, I had to learn that my significance comes from God—not from others.

■ ■ ■

Significance comes from God. Whether we get the job done well or not, we still have value in the eyes of God. We are his children, and nothing that we do or don't do can separate us from his love. On our good days and on our bad days, we still have value in his sight. We can't afford to find our value in others' opinions of us.

► JONATHAN

It's funny: before I had a book published, I'd tell people I was a writer, and people would look at me like, "Yeah, right." I know they secretly pitied my wife, realizing she must live in abject poverty.

But once I got a book published, people seemed to think I was famous or important. They assumed I'm doing well financially. They even asked for my scrawl of a signature after they bought a copy of my book.

People think that getting a book published makes you something. But the truth is, that means absolutely nothing if nobody buys it. It only means I had the right connections, had a reasonable chance at selling copies, and was easy to work with. Monetarily, I'll probably make less money per hour of work than I do on any of my other projects. Unless you're a best-selling author, writing a book takes too long to put together for the probable return on investment. Yet, one little published book somehow gave me credibility.

■ ■ ■

So many people think of significance and value in the wrong terms. They think a published book means something. A title or degree means something. A pat on the back from the pastor means something. And yes, those things have value. But they don't have as much to do with significance as you think. So many of those things are just measures of perseverance and being in the right place at the right time.

Stop looking to those things for your value. There's nothing wrong with wanting to publish a book. With wanting to get a degree or title attached to your name. With wanting the pat on the back from your ministry leader. But if you think those things make you somebody, you'll never be happy. Those things don't mean all that much.

Your value is more than what other people say about you. It's more than outward symbols of success. Seek God first. Seek his righteousness. Then all the other stuff will come along—the value, the significance. You're bigger than your job. You have value, right now, regardless of what you may feel. Start seeing that significance and you can start making your team feel significant. The come back effect starts with you.

KEY POINTS and TAKEAWAYS

1. The key to a strong team is each member understanding their own significance—both as an individual and in their role.
2. Volunteering for a church shouldn't create a sense of obligation or guilt.
3. Feeling significant is often the thing that turns an unmotivated worker into the most motivated person on the team.

4. The evolution of significance in each team member should look like this: (a) they matter in their tasks, (b) they matter apart from their role, and finally (c) they simply matter.

5. Significance comes from God. On our good days and on our bad days, we still have value in his sight. We can't afford to find our value in others' opinions of us.

Appendix

Example Psychographic Sheet

This is a sample psychographic target sheet for Grace Avenue Church in San Antonio, Texas. It's a seven-year-old church with about six hundred people in attendance. In order to better understand the typical attendee at Grace Avenue Church, the team created two fictitious people: Ashley and Chris Smith. They don't represent any one person from the church. But if you met these people walking around San Antonio, Texas, there's a good chance they'd fit right in at the church.

The two personas help the staff and volunteers focus their efforts to make sure everything they do is on target. They plan events for these personas. Make marketing decisions for them. Plan worship sets that will help them best engage. And gear all of their experiences to make these people feel at home.

The primary target is Ashley Smith. Focusing on Ashley and Chris turns the church into a well-kept place that feels more like a party than a stuffy institution. The atmosphere at the church is friendly, fun, and approachable.

Primary Target: Ashley Smith

Age: 32 years old

Location: Northwest San Antonio

Relationship Status: Married for nine years

Children: Three kids, ages 7, 5, and 2

Housing: Owns two-story home

Education: Community college, majored in liberal arts

Employment: Stay-at-home mom, but sells related to her hobby (Etsy or MLM—nutritional supplements or essential oils)

Vehicle: Drives SUV, financed

Finances: Not a lot of discretionary income, but fairly generous

Social Life/Activities: Family-centric entertainment; parks, hiking, and sporting events—watching and attending

Favorite Magazines: *Food Network Magazine*, *HGTV Magazine*

Favorite TV Shows: *Fixer Upper*, *Gilmore Girls*, *Dancing with the Stars*

Shopping: Old Navy, Target, Gap, Starbucks

Social Media: Strong use of Facebook and Instagram. Uses Snapchat more as a novelty than a major source of communication. Pinterest is a huge source of inspiration. Reads healthy living and mommy blogs online.

Primary Need: Wanting to raise their kids in a godly way while also providing financial stability for the family. Wants connection and empowerment.

Church Background: Raised in a church where pressure and legalism were dominant. Was very active in volunteering.

Music: Top 40 and worship music. Listens to Pandora and Spotify.

Interests: Crafting, home décor, healthy cooking, natural remedies, meeting up with the girls for coffee

Secondary Target: Chris Smith

Age: 33 years old

Location: Northwest San Antonio

Relationship Status: Married for nine years

Children: Three kids, ages 7, 5, and 2

Housing: Owns two-story home

Education: Graduated from UTSA with a bachelor's degree in business

Employment: Upwardly mobile in a managerial position. Has the desire to start his own business but doesn't know where to begin.

Vehicle: Drives a Jeep and enjoys working on it on the weekends

Finances: Family finances are stressed but aren't a primary focus

Social Life/Activities: A few friends, mainly interest-based around sports, fitness, or vehicles. Otherwise most time is spent with the family.

Favorite Magazines: Digital only: Gizmodo, Engadget, Unilad, Lifehacker

Favorite TV Shows: Sports and shows from streaming networks

Shopping: Wife primarily does the shopping

Social Media: Some Facebook and Instagram use, primarily for entertainment. Doesn't post too much except for things he finds humorous.

Primary Need: Feels the pressure of providing for family and also being the spiritual head of the home. Wants to take bigger risks and increase his social network but doesn't know where to start.

Church Background: Attended denominational church irregularly as a child

Music: Primarily alternative rock—artists like Keane and Switchfoot. Some worship music: Hillsong United and Elevation Worship.

Interests: Having a good lawn and well-maintained car, fitness, and camping/hunting on the weekends

Notes

Chapter 2 Create a Culture, Not a Job Title

1. Philip Kosloski, "10 Inspiring Quotes from Saint Anthony," *Aleteia*, June 13, 2016, https://aleteia.org/2016/06/13/10-inspiring-quotes-from-saint-anthony /#sthash.ZaCSRtiX.dpuf.

2. "Workplace Culture: What It Is, Why It Matters, & How to Define It," ERC HR Insights Blog, March 6, 2013, http://www.yourerc.com/blog/post/Workplace -Culture-What-it-Is-Why-it-Matters-How-to-Define-It.aspx.

Chapter 3 Know the Guest

1. http://www.merriam-webster.com/dictionary/psychographics.

2. Jairo Senise, "Who Is Your Next Customer?" Strategy+business.com, August 29, 2007, http://www.strategy-business.com/article/07313?_ref=http://en.wikipe dia.org/wiki/Psychographi.

3. Under those questions, we ask more questions to gauge where people are. We also ask these three questions on our guest card. As we walk a guest to his/her seat, we mention how valuable their feedback is right after the service. If they are willing, they answer the three questions and give it to any guest services volunteer.

4. Tony Morgan is a leadership coach/consultant who helps churches with strategic planning and sustained health. He has a great article on his website from which we adapted these problem-solving questions: "Don't Blame Your Staff! 6 Steps to Fixing Broken Church Systems," September 19, 2017, Tony Morgan Live, tonymorganlive.com/2017/09/19/fixing-broken-church-systems.

Chapter 4 Be Fully Present

1. Gordan Peerman, *Blessed Relief: What Christians Can Learn from Buddhists about Suffering* (Woodstock, VT: SkyLight Paths, 2008), 6.

2. Eric Wargo, "How Many Seconds to a First Impression?," Association for Psychological Science, *Observer*, July 2006, http://www.psychologicalscience .org/index.php/publications/observer/2006/july-06/how-many-seconds-to-a-first -impression.html.

Chapter 6 Recover Quickly

1. Holly Stiel, *The Art and Science of the Hotel Concierge* (Orlando, FL: Educational Institute, 2013), 212.

Chapter 7 Observe Details, Because Everything Communicates

1. Joseph Michelli, *The Starbucks Experience* (New York: McGraw-Hill Education, 2006), 54.
2. Matthew May, "The Story behind the Famous FedEx Logo, and Why It Works," Co.Design newsletter, October 23, 2012, http://www.fastcodesign.com /1671067/the-story-behind-the-famous-fedex-logo-and-why-it-works.

Chapter 9 Choose Values over Policies

1. Dale Carnegie, *How to Win Friends and Influence People* (New York: First Pocket Books, 1982), 242.

Jason Young is a hospitality, leadership, and emotional intelligence coach and communicator. He is director of guest experience at Buckhead Church and North Point Ministries, a nationally known network of churches with 36,000 people in average weekly attendance. He has also worked with numerous organizations, including Ford Motor Company, Life.Church, and Chick-fil-A. Jason has written for numerous publications and enjoys posting helpful content at jasonyounglive.com. He lives in Atlanta, Georgia.

Jonathan Malm runs SundaySocial.tv and ChurchStageDesign Ideas.com—reaching more than 70,000 church leaders each month. He has begun multiple businesses and consults with churches regularly on guest services and creative expression. Jonathan had the privilege of directing Echo Conference in 2013, a church conference with over 1,000 attendees. He lives in San Antonio, Texas, and roasts his own coffee beans. Jonathan's first church leadership book, *Unwelcome*, is available on Amazon in print and digital forms.

JASON YOUNG

Hospitality, Leadership, and Emotional Intelligence Coach and Communicator

JasonYoungLive.com

AVAILABLE FOR:

- Personal or Team Coaching
- Keynote Talks
- Church Service Messages
- Half- and Full-Day Workshops

✉ JY@JasonYoungLive.com

§SUNDAYSOCIAL.TV

SundaySocial.tv (a resource from Jonathan Malm) creates at least two new graphics each day for your church to use on social media. There's a verse-of-the-day graphic that mirrors the Bible App's verse and tons of content to help your church get more likes, comments, shares, retweets, and more. Get instant access for a low monthly cost.

CHURCH <u>STAGE DESIGN</u> IDEAS

Looking to update your church stage? Check out this free resource from Jonathan Malm, where hundreds of churches from around the world share pictures of and do-it-yourself information about their own church stages. Visit **churchstagedesignideas.com** to see.

"Pining Away" by Andrew Hunt

"Glowing Hives" by Echo Church

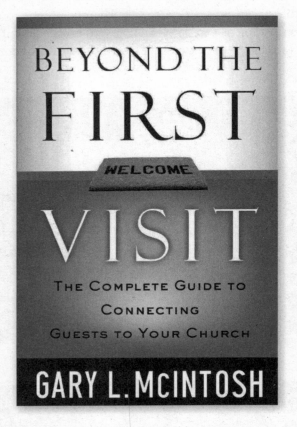